Crescent Color Guide to
Ships

Crescent Color Guide to
Ships
Michael Leitch

Crescent Books
New York

Copyright © The Hamlyn Publishing Group Limited MCMLXXXI

First English edition published by The Hamlyn Publishing Group Limited London · New York · Sydney · Toronto Astronaut House, Feltham, Middlesex, England

Library of Congress Catalog Card Number: ISBN: 0-517-34187-5

This edition is published by Crescent Books, a division of Crown Publishers, Inc. a b c d e f g h

Printed in Italy

Photographic acknowledgments

Animal Graphics, 26 top, 26 bottom left, 26 bottom right; Stewart Bale, Liverpool 44-45; P.G. Boxhall 10 top; British Library, London 17; British Tourist Authority, London 27, 72 top; British Petroleum, London 67 top; Central Press, London 78 top, 78 bottom; Colourviews, Birmingham 40, 40-41, 41, 42; Cooper-Bridgeman Library, London 30, 34 top; Mary Evans Picture Library, London 31 top, 33 top, 33 centre, 37, 39, 57; Exeter Maritime Museum 10 bottom, 33 bottom; Hamlyn Group Picture Library 6, 24 top, 25 top, 31 bottom, 35, 51; Hoverlloyd, London 72 bottom; Robert Hunt Library, London 60, 61 bottom; Imperial War Museum, London 61 centre; Robin Knox-Johnson 79; MARS-Crown copyright (MOD-RAF) 65 bottom, MARS-Danish State Railways 75 top, MARS-McDonnell Douglas Corporation, Texas 66 bottom, MARS-US Navy 66 top, MARS-J.Winkley 16, 71 bottom, 73 top, 73 bottom, 74 top, 74 bottom, 75 centre; National Maritime Museum, Greenwich 19, 22 top, 22 bottom, 23, 24 bottom, 25 bottom, 50-51, 52-53, 55 top, 55 bottom, 56, 58-59, 59, 76; National Scheepvaartmuseum, Antwerp 18; Overseas Containers Ltd, London 70 top, 70 bottom; Photographie Giraudon, Paris 13; Picturepoint, London 9, 11, 12, 34 bottom, 47, 64, 65 top; Popperfoto, London 62 top, 62 bottom, 67 bottom, 68 top, 68 bottom, 69; Rex Features, London 21 top, 29 top, 29 bottom, 46, 80 left, 80 right; Science Museum, London 36; Spectrum Colour Library, London 7 top, 7 bottom, 8, 14 top, 14 bottom, 15, 43, 48-49, 71 top, 75 bottom; Syndication International, London 77; John Topham Picture Library, Edenbridge 61 top, 63 top, 63 bottom.

The illustration on p.20 is reproduced by courtesy of the Master and Fellows of Magdalene College, Cambridge.

Front cover: The *Iberia* (N. V. Robinson). Back cover: The *Cutty Sark*. Title spread: The *Franconia* (N. V. Robinson). Contents spread: The *QE2* (N. V. Robinson).

Contents

When the World Was Small   6

Great Days of Sail   17

Commercial Steam   30

Fighting Ships   50

Special-Purpose Ships   67

Alone Against the Oceans   76

When theWorld Was Small

THE MEDITERRANEAN AND NEAR EAST

The primitive moles and breakwaters of northern Europe now rate as ancient, but we must go back at least twice as far in time, and 20° south in latitude, to find the origins of ships and the science of sailing them. By the fertile shores of the Nile, where the Egyptians founded a brilliant civilization, the first working craft were built.

The Egyptians had little timber, apart from acacia and sycamore which provided only short blocks, so they experimented with papyrus, the paper reed, lumping and binding it into tubular bundles to make elongated rafts, narrowed at the ends or stems which were turned up and bound with cloth or leather. Propulsion was solely by paddle at first, then around 3500 B.C. a small rectangular sail was rigged forward on a bipod mast to take advantage of the wind that habitually blows up the Nile. For downstream voyages, paddles were the only solution for a ship's master wishing to go faster than the current would naturally take him. He, meanwhile, if he had any sense, directed his crew from the shade of a small deckhouse mounted aft; steering was by a larger paddle lashed over the stern.

It is surprising enough to find that papyrus boats, identical in many respects to those of the Ancient Egyptians, can still be seen at work today. What is still more surprising is that one of the places where they are to be found is on the other side of the world, on remote Lake Titicaca in the uplands of Peru. They also sail on Lake Chad, on the far side of the Sahara, and the Ethiopian hobolo, made of a balsa-type wood, must be counted a near-relation. But the presence of a twin boat on a lake in the Andes defies certain explanation. For centuries our mapmakers have told us that in 3000 B.C. the civilized world was confined to the eastern Mediterranean. The papyrus rafts must therefore be a rare instance of independent development. Or must they? One man doubted this explanation enough to risk his life by sailing a raft made of Peruvian balsa logs 5,000 miles across the Pacific. He was the Norwegian scientist Thor Heyerdahl and his landfall in 1947 with this crew of five on an island to the east of Tahiti upset many centuries of conventional wisdom. His raft, the *Kon-Tiki*, named after an Inca god, is now preserved in Oslo. Heyerdahl did not

Right: The mystery of where reed boats began may never be solved. The Egyptians were probably first, but reed vessels also sailed on lakes in South America long before records were kept, and they are still built today. These boats were photographed near Puno in Peru.

The earliest ships of Ancient Egypt had the long slender shape of this model of a funeral barque, and were made of papyrus, the paper reed, or short blocks of wood. The uptilted ends were covered with leather or cloth and some were extravagantly decorated.

conclusively prove that the early Americans had colonized Polynesia all those years before, but he did establish the possibility that trans-oceanic migrations may have taken place, and with them dynamic exchanges of knowledge, on a scale that has yet to be computed.

One crucial fact borne out by the *Kon-Tiki* voyage was that craft made of such lightweight materials had an inbuilt flaw – they leaked. The Ancient Egyptians must have known this too and their next advance was to build stronger craft. At first they used blocks of acacia pegged together, then harder woods from the Upper Nile and cedarwood from the Lebanon. These early sea-going ships were essentially enlarged versions of the reed boats. They were of shallow draught or flat-bottomed. The planks were laid flush and secured together laterally by ribs of rope which were passed in and out of them through slots. The deck cross-beams provided the necessary outward thrust, and the hulls were further strengthened by a double belt of rope running round the outer side and by a hogging truss. This was a stout rope which passed overhead down the centreline of the ship on fork-shaped struts and was fastened at bow and stern to keep either from drooping in a hostile sea.

The mast was still a bipod, fortified by cross-battens, and the sail was tall and rectangular. Artists of the day showed the sails of these square-riggers flat, or side-on, in their wall paintings and carvings, and for a truer impression the reader should imagine the sail turned through 90°, to catch the wind at right-angles to the hull. When the sails were not needed, the mast was lowered aft into an H-shaped rest. Ships bound for Crete or the Lebanon, or down the Red Sea to the land of Punt, had up to fifteen oarsmen on either side. Both prow and stern were decorated with symbols such as a 'magic' eye to repel evil spirits and enemy raiders. Methods of steering varied between two teams of three, working with paddles on either side of the stern, and just two men, one on each side. The tendency was towards fewer men and larger paddles or sweeps. Local craft for journeys on the more placid Nile were fitted

Reed boats with slatted sail, also made of reeds, on Lake Titicaca, Peru. To make this kind of hull, bundles of papyrus are bound into tubes and lashed together.

7

Left: A squat lateen-rigged cargo boat – with the distinctive long sloping yard of its type – works the Nile between El Till and Beni Hassan.

This detail on a Phoenician sarcophagus shows a trading galley from Sidon in the 2nd century B.C. The small sail set on the forward-raked mast was taken up by the Romans who called it the artemon.

out to suit the owner's requirements. There were luxury ships with a large cabin amidships, covered by a canvas or linen awning, and short-run cargo ships with an open-top pen for containing grain or livestock.

Around 1500 B.C. the initiative in the Mediterranean passed to the Phoenicians. Operating out of the world's first major ports at Tyre and Sidon, they were avid traders who fetched and carried across vast areas. Where the Egyptians had preferred to hug the coastline – just as the longshore fishing craft continued to do in the 19th century – the Phoenicians were less fearful of blank horizons. That they circumnavigated Africa has been suggested though not proved, but they almost certainly passed through the Straits of Gibraltar (in Classical times called the Pillars of Hercules) and turned north, going as far as the 'tin islands' of Western Britain – probably the Scillies. They had two basic kinds of ship – a long galley-type for fighting, which we shall meet later, and what the Greeks called *gauloi*, or tubs. These were beamy traders, in shape rather like half a pear, and they carried more sail than the lean war galleys.

The Phoenicians were shipbuilders to the known world and their designs were successively absorbed by the Greeks and the Romans. Over the centuries there were gradual improvements in handling techniques. Brails threaded through the mainsail made it easier to shorten sail from the bottom in a high wind. Ships' lengths increased from roughly 70 feet (21·3 metres) in Egyptian times to 100 feet (30·5 metres) by the heyday of the Romans; by then cargo capacities were up to about 250 tons and the ships were fully decked, the cargo being stowed below in holds.

9

Above: The sturdy
lines of a dhow local
to the Malabar Coast
of India.

Left: When this
pearling dhow from
Bahrain goes about,
fifteen men are
needed to push the
heavy yards forward
and round the masts.

Three important advances were made in the Greco-Roman period. One was the development of the stern in the form of a primitive aftercastle. Using this extra height the rudderman could exert greater leverage; he now stood on a bridge and directed both sweeps with the aid of tillers attached to the tops of each.

The other advances had to do with sails and rigs. From vases, grave-paintings and wooden models, we can see the emergence of new sails. First a pair of triangular topsails was set above the yard, or upper beam supporting the mainsail. They gave additional power in light winds. The Romans introduced a further square sail, rigged over the bows on a forward-tilting mast and known as the artemon. Its primary use was to keep the ship before the wind and so make steering easier.

Shipbuilders in Abu Dhabi shape the hull of a dhow, the classic Arab sailing vessel.

More revolutionary was the latine or lateen sail. Though the Arabs are usually credited with its invention, there is evidence that the Greeks knew and employed it at an earlier date. The great breakthrough with the lateen is in its flexibility. The sail is triangular, laced to a slanting yard and can be swung through blocks and tackles to catch the wind from almost astern to almost side-on, when it is in a near fore-and-aft position. In the Aegean, ships for the first time could progress against the wind by filling their mainsail on alternate sides of the ship, moving forward in a zig-zag path or tack.

When taken up by the Arab nations as well as by the peoples of the northern Mediterranean, the lateen idea was the source of a family of cargo ships, designed mostly for river and coastal work. One of the most unexpected shapes is the double lateen of the Nile gaiassa, a survivor to this day. The gaiassa has two short masts and tall lateen sails attached to long yards that droop at the upper end, like the wings of a gull at the top of its flapping cycle. Gaiassas, like many other lateens working in reliably calm waters, have a shallow draught.

The Western name for the classic Arab lateen is the dhow. Many types evolved to suit particular waters and functions – the ferry boats of the Upper Nile, the shallow-draught traders of the Red Sea and the Persian Gulf, among them the baghla and the zaruk, used alike by above-board commodity merchants, by ivory smugglers and pearl-divers.

NORTHERN EUROPE

East Gotland has a far colder climate; it forms part of southern Sweden. Early rock paintings from East Gotland indicate a long seafaring tradition even before these Northern people were attacked by marauding Roman galleys advancing up the North Sea. These Northerners were the Vikings, and in their long war with the sea they had come to different conclusions about its conquest. They built long beamy trading ships with high angled stem and stern posts, the single mast carrying a rectangular sail of chequered appearance, probably because it had diagonal strips, possibly of leather, reinforcing the basic homespun material.

Two discoveries in the last century have shown us more than we ever knew before about Viking ships. In 1880 at Gokstad, Sweden, a 10th-century merchant ship was unearthed from the blue clay of that district. She was in fine condition and was soon established as a karv, a double-ended coastal trader, about 77 feet (23·4 metres) long and 16 feet 6 inches (5 metres) at the broadest point. These comparative measurements differ markedly, with their ratio of about 5 to 1, from those of the rounder Mediterranean ships, where a proportion of 3 to 1 was common.

The other find was in 1904 at Oseberg, Norway, where another broad-beamed trader was uncovered. Older by about a century than the Gokstad ship, she too was clinker-built in the Northern style with the planks overlapping. In the Mediterranean, ships were carvel-built with the planks laid flush and the gaps sealed with hemp and pitch. When not under sail, the Oseberg ship was rowed by fifteen pairs of oars.

There is evidence enough to reconstruct one of the longer Viking war galleys, but a real missing link in the story of North Sea ships is the knorr. The

Broad in the beam with a high prow and stern post, this vessel in the Viking Ship Museum near Oslo is typical of the Nordic coastal traders of the 10th-11th centuries.

The nef of St. Ursula, made in the late 15th century and now kept in the Cathedral Treasury at Rheims. Nefs were enlarged versions of the medieval cog, a round-bellied trading type. The name was transferred to elegant table ornaments, made in the form of ships; for dinners and banquets they were loaded with salt and 'sailed' up and down the table.

knorr is said to be the direct ancestor of the Baltic and British traders. Probably broad in the beam, with high cutwaters at stem and stern, she foreshadowed the sudden flowering of merchant shipping associated with the Hanseatic League and its headquarters port, Lübeck.

The League was a mutual protection society formed by German trade interests in the Rhineland and on the Baltic and at its height in the 14th century had some 100 member-towns. Their more positive naval contributions included building lighthouses, training pilots and encouraging the design of better and more efficient ships.

The main new type was the cog, a straight-ended, round-bellied cargo carrier that stood high in the water and was protected at either end by soldiers – archers and swordsmen – who were mustered as needed on fighting platforms known as fore and aftercastles. In time the aftercastles merged with the hull and became the master's quarters, also those of the mate if he was lucky, and accommodated small numbers of well-to-do passengers.

City seals of the early Middle Ages provide almost the only documentation of ships and their evolution at that time both in German and British waters. The Cinque Ports of south-east England were a military foundation, organized in the 11th century to supply the monarch with ships and men. Two further 'head ports' were added later, and round these seven the King's fleet was assembled. Apart from larger castles and fighting tops, there was little difference between war and merchant ships. As the city seals show, it was during this time, from the 12th to the 14th century, that side rudders were exchanged for a single rudder positioned over the stern post and worked by a tiller. First evidence of the stern rudder appears on a 12th-century font made in Belgium and now in Winchester Cathedral.

Right: On Lake Chad, south of the Sahara, reed boats are still found, and numerous examples of the universal dugout – perhaps the most basic form of water transport.

Above: Sanur Beach, Bali, is the home of these dramatic lateen-rigged vessels. Curving from the nearer hull are the supports for the outrigger, which supplies essential stability in turbulent seas.

The cog was generally a single-master, but towards the end of the 14th century the power of the single square sail was increased by a smaller triangular sail on a mast closer to the stern – the mizzen. The shipyards were now set for the technological explosion of the 15th century that culminated in the full-riggers, the galleons, and the 'great ships' that were constructed as much for national propaganda as for their intrinsic worth.

FOLK BOATS OF THE WORLD

We shall meet those maritime monsters in the next chapter. So far we have been mainly Western or Eurocentric in tracing the evolution of ships. Alongside events in Egypt, the Mediterranean and the North Sea, peoples all over the world had been discovering how to make simple boats that could be propelled by paddle or sail. Many were extensions of the hollowed-tree idea, the dugout which became a canoe or kayak, then perhaps grew outriggers for greater stability. Space forbids a grand survey of the numerous local types, but below we look at some of the more representative specimens.

The canoe principle was taken up by civilizations as far apart as Ireland and China. Ox hide was the material favoured by the Irish for their single-masted curraghs, while the Eskimos of North America stretched sealskins around a driftwood frame.

In the Pacific many traditional types have not been superseded, coexisting oddly with the universal motor launch and mechanically powered versions of their original selves. Sailing canoes have retained their slim lines, derived from the narrow shape of a hollowed log. Where bigger craft were needed, the tendency was to make double canoes, some bridged with a cabin, or to add one or more outriggers which allowed larger cargoes to be carried on a bamboo frame stretched above the struts leading to the outriggers.

Giants of the canoe class were the Maoris' tainuis. These were huge double canoes more than 70 feet (21·3 metres) long with a large pitched-roofed cabin amidships. Two bipod masts supported a pair of tall claw-shaped sails. In these craft the Maoris made their great migration across the Pacific from Melanesia-Polynesia to New Zealand. A related type is the New Guinea lakatoi. This usually consists of three canoe hulls jointed by transverse beams; a bamboo platform is then mounted on top. Like the tainui the lakatoi carries two claw-shaped sails.

The word catamaran now describes almost any double-hulled craft. It has narrower origins, though, in the Tamil word meaning 'tied wood or logs' and was first applied in a sailing context to the local craft that worked along the coasts of southern India and Sri Lanka. The aptness of the word is clear to see in the kola maram or 'flying fish catamaran'. Seven logs are tied together, tapering towards the bow where five shorter lengths turn upwards in a primitive prow. To oppose a tendency to drift, leeboards were carried on either side and lowered into the water as needed.

A two-masted junk from Hong Kong. Most notable feature of the Chinese junk is the 'venetian blind' sail, made in panels with supporting cross-battens.

Traditional barco rabelo, used for ferrying casks of port on the River Douro. Steerage is by a huge sweep mounted over the stern – essential for keeping the boat on course through the rapids upstream.

Elaborate to look at as a Burmese temple carving, the Irrawaddy rice boat with billowing sails is one of the most picturesque of all local sailing craft. The upward rake of prow and stern and the curved roof of the deckhouse, often intricately decorated, together with the improbable breadth of the finely balanced yard, conspire to disguise what is at heart a canoe, embellished and refined over the centuries. A further conservative note is struck by the long spade-shaped side rudder.

One final classic type: the junk. The Japanese had one, with an artemon sail very like that of the old Roman grain ships, but it was in mainland China that the junk prospered and released a family of trading ships. At its most primitive, the junk is a shallow rectilinear box, flat-bottomed, divided into watertight compartments – a feature the West was slow to copy – and powered by a square sail. The typical venetian-blind appearance of the junk's sail comes from its panel construction, the linen or matting sail surface supported by bamboo cross-battens. In the more advanced types, such as the Foochow and the Pechili trader, junks had several masts and a lateen-lugsail rig. Pechili junks were up to 180 feet (54·8 metres) long, and the larger ones could carry cargoes of 400 tons. To compensate for the inherent instability of its flat bottom, the hull slanted upwards at the stern and a large inboard rudder descended beneath the level of the flat bottom, to double as a keel.

As long ago as the 9th century, junks were roaming as far as the Indian Ocean and the east coast of Africa. There are those who believe that it was the junk's lugsail that inspired the Arab lateen rig, which then spread west to the Mediterranean. While we incline to credit the shipyards of the northern Mediterranean with the first lateens, there is no doubting the sophistication of the junk's sail. The proven aerodynamic efficiency of the separately operated panels has even influenced the latest generation of windships – the sail-assisted tankers of Japan, the first of which was launched in August 1980.

Great Days of Sail

CARRACK AND CARAVEL

No overnight revelation spurred the shipbuilders of Europe to revolutionize the scope of their trade in the late 14th century. Word travelled too slowly to permit this, but the changes wrought in the space of the next hundred years were sweeping and remarkable. During that time there was a true marriage of the Northern and Mediterranean traditions. From manuscripts, paintings, models and many other sources we know that North Sea cogs trading in the Mediterranean were copied. The square sail and the stern rudder were their distinguishing marks, and to these the Mediterraneans added a small lateen-rigged mizzen.

The Romans had had their forward-raked artemon sail, and now the Southern builders rigged a third mast, stepped on the forecastle, with a square sail. Both the new sails were intended to make steering easier rather than to increase speed through the water, but in handling the increasingly complex arrangements of shrouds the 15th-century sailor must have felt mounting confidence in his power to harness the wind.

The Spanish, Italians and Portuguese who now broke with tradition appreciated the power before the wind of the square-rigged sail. Although it could not sail so close to the wind, it was simpler to man and did not require a team of 15 men to heave up the lateen yard and force it round the other side of the mast on going about. The upshot of these new ideas was a caravel of mixed rigging and three masts. In Northern yards a similar process of revision was under way, culminating in the carrack.

The 'kraek' (carrack) depicted by the Flemish master 'W.A.' was a three-master. Its mixed rig was of a similar pattern to the Southern ships (square main- and foresail, lateen mizzen), and it had extensive fore- and aftercastles covered by awnings. Overhanging the stern was a railed gallery flanked by two box-shaped privies which emulated the privy shafts of medieval castles, positioned above water channels connecting with the moat.

In the years that followed three further sails emerged. Forward of the bows a spritsail was suspended from the bowsprit; a topsail was set on the flagstaff mounted on the top or crow's nest of the mainmast, and aft of the mizzen appeared a smaller fourth mast that carried a lateen-rigged sail – the bona-venture mizzen.

The Earl of Salisbury arrives off Conway Castle aboard a sturdy square-rigged cog. The reef-points for shortening sail are clearly shown in this French manuscript illustration of 1319.

This added sailpower achieved two important ends. It gave the major maritime powers the means to build imposing 'great ships' with up to six decks, able to support a considerable weight of cannon. The Scottish ship *Great Michael* (1511) was rigged in this fashion, and the massive Portuguese flagship *Santa Caterina do Monte Sinai* (1520) was broadly similar, with the addition of a topsail on the foremast, and a square stern tapering skywards armed with several cannon. Henry VIII of England's great ship, the *Henry Grâce à Dieu*, is often cited as the masterwork of her age. She was built in 1514 on the same lines as the previous two, but a major refit in the late 1530s brought considerable enlargement of the sail area, with the forward three masts carrying mainsail, topsail and topgallants. This was achieved by enlarging the tops so that the topmast could support a subsidiary top and a third sail. The arms of the main- and foremast yards had double hooks at each end to catch and rip the rigging and sails of an enemy ship when they closed for the decisive fight at close-quarters.

The second, and greater, leap forward was in the physical range of these powerful carracks. Now men could sail to the far ends of the world, and round it. In 1492 Christopher Columbus, after a decade of argument and frustration, gained the sponsorship he needed from the Spanish royal family, and set off to sail west to 'the Indies'. By this he meant the Far East but, as we now know, the American continent interposed itself together with the group of islands which since those times have been called the West Indies.

What gave Columbus the confidence to override all objections to his grand scheme? As were many Renaissance men, he was fired by the excitement of

In the first half of the 16th century Antwerp was the leading merchant centre of western Europe. In this painting, ships from north and south crowd the approaches to the port.

Right: Ships of mainly Portuguese origin, painted c. 1530 by Cornelius Anthoniszoon. The largest ship, with its towering stern and mixed rig of square and lateen sails, is typical of the carracks then in service.

new knowledge, the evidence of his own eyes, a thorough knowledge of his field, i.e. seamanship, and the conviction that God would see him through his extraordinary undertaking. He had read of Marco Polo's great sea voyage in 1292 from Changchow in China to Persia, and became obsessed with the idea of finding a westward route to the Orient. He was an experienced navigator, and had made voyages round the coast of Africa and, in 1478, north as far as Iceland and possibly Greenland. 'I have made it my business to read all that has been written on geography, history, philosophy and other sciences,' he once declared, 'then Our Lord revealed to me that it was feasible to sail from here to the Indies and placed in me a burning desire to carry out this plan.'

The ships that Columbus took with him were modest indeed compared to the 'great ships', but were superbly built for the unknowns of a long-distance ocean voyage. In Spain they were generically described as *naos*, and the French equivalent word is *nef*, used in English to describe those beautiful silver sailing vessels that adorned the dining tables of the wealthy and in which the salt shuttled back and forth.

Columbus took only 87 men in his three ships. Thirty-nine, or nearly half this number, sailed aboard the flagship *Santa Maria*. She was a merchant caravel assigned to the expedition with her crew of northern Spaniards and her captain-owner Juan de la Cosa. She was about 85 feet (26 metres) long and 25 feet (7·6 metres) in the beam. Her companions were the caravels *Pinta* and *Nina*; the latter was rerigged in the Canary Islands with a square sail on the main- and foremasts.

At least two of the four ships that sailed to India in 1497 with Vasco da Gama also were caravels; a contemporary illustration shows them with topsails on the main- and foremasts. It was also a caravel which made the first circumnavigation of the world. She was the *Vittoria*, sole survivor of the five ships that set out in 1519 under Ferdinand Magellan. The flagship, *Trinidad*, got as far as Borneo, though by then her captain-general was dead, killed in an unnecessary military expedition against the islanders of Mactan in the Philippines. Murder, mutiny, starvation and scurvy continually claimed their victims almost from the outset, and of the 270 men who sailed with Magellan in September 1519 only 31 remained to enjoy the honour of manning the *Vittoria* in July 1522 as she limped into Seville.

THE GALLEON

Both the English and the Spanish lay claim to building the first of the next principal ship type – the galleon. Although the term never became current in England to describe English ships, it is possible that their advanced lines were originally formulated by Elizabeth I's master-shipwright Matthew Baker, appointed in 1572. One of the fundamental differences between the carrack and the galleon was the lowering of the high forecastle, which the English navigator Sir John Hawkins had isolated as an important design flaw in his round voyages to Africa and the West Indies. Because of its height the forecastle tended to pull the ship away from the wind. The galleon that evolved had a shallow forecastle absorbed into the hull, and in front of it was a beakhead from which men could more easily handle the spritsail.

Shipping now took two main directions. The hunger for 'great ships' persisted in the minds of monarchs, and Gustavus Adolphus of Sweden, one of the fathers of warfare in the first age of national armed forces, ordered the building of the *Vasa*. She weighed 1,300 tons, was about 170 feet (50 metres) long and had a beam of about 35 feet (10 metres). With her deep topsails and topgallants she must have been an imposing spectacle as she set off on her maiden voyage in August 1628. She was intended as a warship and carried 64 guns. These and her impressive suit of sails made demands on her stability which her shallow draught of 14 feet (4·2 metres) could not meet when challenged by the first strong winds to meet her as she sailed from Stockholm towards the open sea. She heeled rapidly and sank to the bottom of the estuary with the loss of some fifty lives. In 1961 she was raised to the surface and towed to the dry dock where she now stands preserved.

No such ill-fortune struck Charles I of England's great three-masted ship, *Sovereign of the Seas*, designed by Phineas Pett and launched at Woolwich in 1637. She was the largest ship of her day: 1,522 tons, 232 feet (70·6 metres) in overall length, 46 feet (14 metres) in the beam and with a draught of 22 feet (6·6 metres). With her royals – a new sail – rigged above the topgallants on fore- and mainmast, she was the grandest of Britain's three 1st Rate ships listed in Vice-Admiral William Batten's Fleet Survey of 1642. She was then judged fit for 15 years' more service, but she in fact survived until 1696 when she was accidentally destroyed by fire at Chatham. She proved a valiant war-

Below: Henry VIII's 'great ship' the *Henry Grâce à Dieu*, pictured in the Anthony Rolls of 1545 after her major refit in the 1530s. She was armed with 151 bronze and iron guns and 100 hand guns.

Right: The Elizabethan navigators crossed the world's oceans in ships that were relatively modest – like the *Golden Hind* shown here in reconstruction. In 1577-80 Francis Drake circumnavigated the globe in her, and afterwards was knighted on board by the Queen.

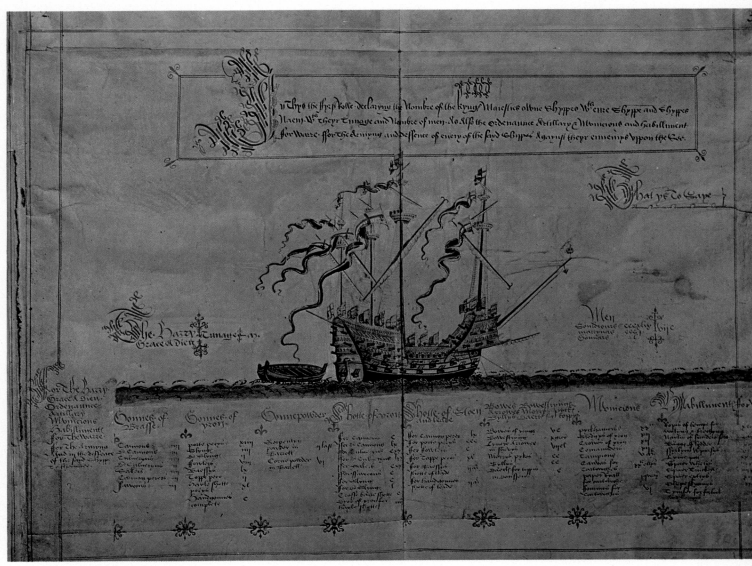

ship against the Dutch fleet, and from the enemy took the nickname 'Golden Devil', a backhanded tribute to the mass of gilded carving, also called 'gingerbread', which adorned her mountainous stern and hull sides. In 1660 she was given a major refit and thereafter was known as the *Royal Sovereign*.

The evolution of sails and rigging reached a temporary peak with the *Sovereign of the Seas*, and it is interesting to pause here and consider just what had been going on in the 250 years since the humble single-masted cog began the first of its many transformation. Although the *Sovereign of the Seas* might have had four rather than three masts, great use was made of the bowsprit, and the sails on the masts proper are complex enough. From bow to stern, bottom to top, she carried the following sails:

Bowsprit: Spritsail and spritsail topsail.

Foremast: Foresail with bonnet (an easily removable extra strip of sail attached to the foot of the main section); fore topsail; fore topgallant; fore royal.

Mainmast: Mainsail with bonnet; main topsail; main topgallant; main royal.

Mizzen: Mizzen with bonnet (lateen-rigged; all the other sails were square-rigged, suspended from horizontal yards); mizzen topsail; mizzen topgallant.

To this expansive layout would soon be added staysails and studding sails. Staysails were triangular and were rigged fore and aft from the tops. The studding sails were rigged on either side of the topsails, giving extra width at the second level and laced to extension booms on the yardarm.

Other ships of the galleon type were commissioned for service with the British and Dutch East India Companies, formed in the early 1600s to exploit the spice trade in Far Eastern lands. To make greater cargo room while not cutting back on necessary defensive armament, the East Indiamen took on a relatively stout appearance. Whatever they lacked in speed, they were survivors and in ever-larger form lasted until the 1850s, when merchant shipping entered its final and most dynamic phase with the clippers.

AFTER THE MAYFLOWER

The technological explosion that created the full-rigger spread outward to all ranks of shipping and influenced the shape of numerous more modest traders. A prominent type was the fluyt, of Dutch origin, known in her English form

Phineas Pett, proud architect of the *Sovereign of the Seas*, Charles I's great prestige ship launched in 1637. The Dutch Navy knew her as the 'Golden Devil' from the wealth of gilded carving or 'gingerbread' cladding her stern and hull sides.

Right: A trading brig enters the Avon en route for the port of Bristol in 1838. She carries a typically mixed rig, with two square-rigged masts, a gaff-and-boom brigsail aft, triangular staysail and forward jib set on an extension to the bowsprit—the jib-boom.

as the flyboat. These were three-masters, with a rounded stern and a flat bottom, and it was in a ship of this type that the Pilgrim Fathers sailed on 6 September 1620 from Plymouth, crossing the Atlantic to Provincetown Harbor, on the northern tip of Cape Cod, which they reached on 11 November.

In 1957 Alan Villiers took a replica of that historic ship, the *Mayflower*, on a commemorative voyage along the same route. He later wrote approvingly of the steady way she handled. The lateen-rigged mizzen he found 'awkward', but he also found that the spritsail, set far ahead on the long bowsprit, was a sail of such effectiveness in manoeuvre that he wondered why it had ever been given up for the less efficient jibs.

The jib became a feature of 18th-century ships, ousting the square-rigged topsail on the bowsprit. The bowsprit was extended by means of a jib-boom, enabling two triangular fore-and-aft sails to be set in line on the stays of the foremast. In later years, the higher sails climbed the more jibs could be set. In the 19th century a ship with four sails on the foremast could carry four jibs; outermost was the flying jib, then the outer jib, the inner jib and the jib.

The opening of the East to western merchants was largely brought about by the British and Dutch East India Companies from 1600. Here the return to Amsterdam of four Dutch ships is recorded by Andries van Eertvelt.

In common with the fluyt the fighting frigate retained the now-traditional beak-head, as did the square-sterned pinnace, the hagboat and the pink, whereas it was discarded in the blunt-nosed cat and the barque. This profusion of hull types is initially bewildering, but reflects the strong-mindedness of shipbuilders who designed ships to suit the waters they would be used in. An important and lasting innovation came with the brigsail, gaff-rigged on a spar running aft of the mainmast. This effectively did away with the troublesome lateen-rigged mizzen.

The gaff-rigged sail gained favour from Dutch inland waters to the shores of Massachusetts and was soon to be found on both fore- and mainmasts of the *bezaan jacht* (a Dutch term) and the schooner, which was of American origin. Even in Mediterranean waters, where the Barbary pirates did brisk business in their fast commerce-raiding chebecks, the gaffsail made an impression. Various local Portuguese craft adopted the gaff rig, and the spritsail also gained favour; examples range from the Thames sailing barge to the Greek scapho and sacoleva, and the Turkish tchektirme. Much the same process of moving away from square to fore-and-aft rig was to be found in the fishing fleets, where versions of the ketch, cutter and yawl lifted immense catches of fish from the rich grounds of the North Sea and the Iceland Banks.

CLIPPERS AND GIANTS

The original of the clipper ship was a schooner. These early became a speciality of the Baltimore yards, and took the name of Baltimore clipper. They were narrow, fast, and 'clipped down the wind', and in the 1820s and '30s, when steam was beginning to make its presence felt, they were the ideal response of men determined to stay with canvas.

Baltimore clippers, also referred to as Baltimore packets, commandeered the Atlantic routes from 1816, when the Black Ball Line opened a regular service with four 500-tonners. On the East Indian routes, a bulkier vessel

Brown-sailed Thames sailing barges in one of their regular summer races. Now retired, these were the staple traders of the Thames Estuary and east coast of England.

23

resembling a man of war, the Blackwall frigate, made its presence felt.

But the steamship was fast making ground. The 1840s were a critical decade. Not only was Brunel's screw-powered *Great Britain* of 1845 the largest ship of her day, she offered object lessons in strength and reliability. Then, in the same year, the advocates of sail struck back with the launch in New York of the *Rainbow*, the first true clipper. Her towering rig incorporated all the latest thinking, with three jibs and a gaffsail (the spanker) aft of the mizzen. What most took the eye were the six square-rigged sails on both fore- and mainmast, and a further five on the mizzen, forward of the spanker.

Ships of the *Rainbow* type were built by many lines, and by their speed became queens of the long-distance ocean routes. The tea- and spice-producing nations of the Far East had no comparable large ships for exporting their goods to Europe. The clipper ship proved for the time being ideal for this trade, and for carrying wool from Australia. Further impetus was provided by the California Gold Rush and by the passing in Britain of the Customs Consolidation Act of 1853, which allowed foreign ships to handle British trade on equal terms.

Clippers were the racehorses of the ocean, and owners encouraged the masters to compete for speed with rival ships. A classic race to be first home with the new tea crop was set up between the *Ariel*, *Taiping* and *Serica*, from Foochow to London. Setting off on 30 May 1866 the three ships sailed across the South China Sea and the Indian Ocean down to the Cape of Good Hope. None of the ships had much idea where the others were, and each skipper gleaned what he could from passing vessels. On 29 August, after 91 days, all three ships passed the Azores. *Serica* kept more to the French coast as they entered the Channel, and lost ground, but *Taiping* and *Ariel* were still neck and neck in the Thames Estuary. All three caught the same tide into London, and after 16,000 miles *Taiping* was first home by 20 minutes. Another ship on the China–London run, the *Fiery Cross*, set a record for a day's run by logging 328 nautical miles in one 24-hour period.

For some 30 years the world thrilled to the deeds of the flying clippers. Largest wooden clipper was the American *Great Republic*, launched in 1853. She was 325 feet (99 metres) long, with a beam of 53 feet (16·2 metres) and holds 38 feet (11·5 metres) deep. In her original form she had a massive suit of 33 sails, but was never allowed to demonstrate her full potential. A fire, the

Far left top: The *Mount Stewart*, a British wool clipper built in 1891 for the Australian trade: painting by J. Spurling.

Far left bottom: The clipper ship *Lahloo*, built in 1867. Her hull is unmistakably that of an ocean racer, sharply raked at stem and stern to minimize contact with the water.

Below: A Leith fishing smack with all sails set, recorded in 1838 by J. C. Schetky.

Bottom: Together after 16,000 miles, the clippers *Taiping* and *Ariel* race up the English Channel on the last leg of their race in 1866 from Foochow.

This page: The oldest merchantman afloat today. Such is the boast of the current owners of the *Star of India*, a barque of 1,197 tons first launched in 1863 as *Euterpe* and now preserved in San Diego, California.

Right: Graceful survivors at Plymouth Sound in a Tall Ships Race.

seaman's worst enemy, broke out shortly before her maiden voyage, and in the substantial refit she was considerably reduced in both hull and rig.

The quest for greater speed brought about the demise of the clipper, since it could only be achieved by streamlining the hull. This meant cutting back on cargo space, and ultimately the clipper became uneconomic. The opening of the Suez Canal in 1869 led to the steamships collaring the China tea trade, and clippers were switched to the Australia route. Here, as with the South American nitrate and guano trades, it was found that certain larger ships brought greater returns and required less manning. These were scaled-up barques with up to five masts, generally square-rigged with jibs and a gaff-rigged mizzen. Iron and steel hulls gave them massive strength and endurance, and for a while the oceans witnessed some extraordinary mammoths.

There was the German 5,100-ton *Preussen*, launched in 1902, the world's only five-masted full-rigger. She was 438 feet (133·5 metres) long, with a beam of 54 feet (16·4 metres), and she was one of the famous Flying P line which worked between Chile and Hamburg. Other of the line's great ships, whose names all started with the letter P, were the *Passat* and the *Potosi*.

There was also the unique *Thomas W Lawson* (1902), a vast steel-hulled schooner with seven masts. She was the culminating point in the development of the monster sailing ship as a bulk carrier able to compete profitably with the steamships – profitable because of her capacity and because she needed only 12 men, aided by steam winches, to work her sails. After World War I it was clear that mechanization must eventually sweep the seas, and although some large vessels remained in service as offshore traders and plied the Great Lakes of North America, and some lived on as training ships, the effective end of the sail-driven cargo ship had come.

CAN SAIL RETURN?

Purists might argue that commercial sail has never entirely gone away, but such arguments must largely rely for evidence on rare survivors of bygone days. It was with some astonishment, therefore, that TV viewers in August 1980 found themselves watching the launch of a 1,600-ton Japanese tanker, the *Shinaitoku Maru*. On the usually blank acreage of the deck reared two masts enclosed by an elongated triangular casing. This turned out to be a hinged rigid sail. When folded out, its panels resembled a gigantic blind. In operation, the angle of the sail to the wind can be power-adjusted, and the whole contraption folds away when the wind is unfavourable.

Since the oil-producing countries of the Middle East sent the price of oil sky high in the mid-1970s, oil conservation has become of paramount importance to thousands of manufacturing companies. The *Shinaitoku Maru* demonstrates one Japanese shipping company's way of tackling the problem. On present estimates, these rigid auxiliary sails can produce a 10 per cent oil saving. As yet this is not enough to cover their costs and the consequent loss of cargo capacity caused by their weight. However, the company responsible, Nippon Kokan, reason that the price of oil will go on rising and that the venture should soon pay its way. Nor will it be limited to ships of the *Shinaitoku Maru*'s modest capacity. The system can be scaled up for fitting to ships of at least 20,000 tons, at which point the sails would be 120 feet (36·4 metres) high and 75 feet (22·8 metres) wide.

Nippon Kokan reached their present conclusions after trying out three different systems of auxiliary sail on a test barge shaped like an oil tanker in miniature. One was triangular, and one consisted largely of a framed rectangle of soft canvas; the chosen version operates three columns of framed panels, the central one being rigid and the outer 'wings' made of canvas.

A parallel venture developed at Hamburg University in the 1950s and now under scrutiny in the United States is the Dynaship. This has yet to be proved on any meaningful scale, but envisaged is a ship with six massively thick 200-foot (60-metre) masts each carrying five sails on yards. The yards would operate like curtain tracks, and at the push of a control button on the bridge the sails would glide along the yards. Instead of being furled in the customary vertical direction when not required, the sails would be made to vanish – into a storage cylinder inside the mast.

The giant mast recalls an invention of the 1920s – Flettner's rotor ship.

Left and above: A true wonder of the energy-conscious 1980s is this Japanese tanker, the *Shinaitoku Maru*. Her two power-adjusted rigid sails fold away at the push of a button. In action, they offer a ten per cent saving on oil fuel and may be the shape of sails to come.

After experimenting successfully on a converted 960-ton schooner, the German engineer Anton Flettner built his rotor ship *Barbara* with two giant cylinders resembling overgrown funnels, each 60 feet (18·2 metres) high. The idea behind the rotor was to spin it with an electric motor. As it rotated, and wind blew across the cylinder, two opposing pressure zones were set up on the sides facing and turned away from the airflow. This caused the cylinder to move in a direction at right-angles to the airflow. The rotors propelled the *Barbara* at a speed of 6 knots in moderate winds; added to the 7 knots provided by the ship's engines, this made her a workable proposition and for some years she served between Hamburg and the River Plate. Flettner's rotor ship remained an oddity, however, and no further work was done on the principle – until recently, when the naval architects of the world were forced by the oil issue to look again at alternative power sources. As yet there have been no commercial moves to reharness the Flettner system, but the fact that, in its day, it worked will not be lost on tomorrow's contractors.

One man who sees the future in the traditional past is an Englishman, Commander Mike Willoughby. He is the force behind the plan to build a gigantic five-masted square-rigger with an overall length of 482 feet (145·8 metres). She would be a cargo ship, and recorded estimates of her building cost vary between £6 million and £12 million. Willoughby's 15,000-tonner would be huge, though not dramatically out of scale with the multi-masters built at the turn of the century like the *Thomas W Lawson*. Here, again, the price of oil has given a government the spur to examine the feasibility of Willoughby's plan. But whether Britain is prepared to invest in more than initial studies remains to be seen. Perhaps the money may come from elsewhere. Meanwhile there is no doubt that it is reasonable to look for savings on oil consumption – and even to plan for the day when there is no more oil. And one of the most obvious directions to look is at a system that worked more than adequately for 5,000 years – the windship.

Commercial Steam

A pioneer steamboat on the Clyde near Dumbarton. She is probably the *Comet*, which from 1812 operated Europe's first regular passenger service, running three times a week from Glasgow to Greenock and back.

Right: The power of steam over sail. Reminiscent of J. M. W. Turner's famous painting of the 'Fighting Téméraire', this view shows a paddle-driven tug towing a brig into harbour: the painting is dated 1897.

THE PIONEERS

To build the first practical steamboat was a challenge that inspired countless inventors in backyard workshops towards the end of the 18th century. Several faltering 'firsts' had advanced the state of the art before William Symington designed the canal tug *Charlotte Dundas* which is the generally acknowledged 'winner', and these earlier efforts deserve credit they do not often receive.

Little is known outside France of Jacques Périer, who in 1775 brought off the first successful trial of a steam-powered boat. Nor outside America of John Fitch, inventor in 1786 of a kind of steam canoe, powered by two lines of six mechanical paddles, but with no commercial function. In 1790 Fitch produced another impractical steamboat called *Experiment*: this ran satisfactorily on the Delaware River, but the bulk of the machinery also used up the space intended for cargo.

Outside Britain there is little interest in Patrick Miller, a Scottish banker who developed a twin-hulled paddle-boat that in 1787 crossed the North Sea to Sweden. Since the paddles had to be worked by hand – a process which soon exhausted the crew – this was no great step forward for the Industrial Revolution. It might even be called a regression, for the Romans in the 6th century A.D. had devised a paddle-ship with wheels turned by oxen harnessed to a treadmill on the deck. (The treadmill idea was not pursued at the time, though in the 19th century 'horse boats' were used to ferry passengers across rivers in the United States, the treadmill being attached to a wheel or wheels at the stern or sides.)

Patrick Miller's greater contribution was to call in the young engineer William Symington, who designed a steam engine for his paddle-wheeler; though primitive, the chain-driven paddles churned rapidly enough to achieve a speed of 5 mph on Dalwinston Loch, Dumfriesshire, in October 1787. That, however, seemed to be the maximum speed for that engine, and Miller, resigned to failure, removed the engine to his house in Edinburgh where it remained, a bulky keepsake of what might have been.

Symington, meanwhile, was determined to build a working steamship. He persuaded the shareholders of the Forth and Clyde Canal that steam-

powered boats would be more profitable than horses for hauling barges on the canal. Lord Dundas sponsored the building at Grangemouth of the *Charlotte Dundas*, named after his daughter. To cut down side-wash, and pressure on the canal banks, Symington produced a double-acting cylinder engine that drove a large stern wheel through a rod and crank. At her trial run, and despite a strong headwind, the *Charlotte Dundas* pulled two 70-ton barges for $19\frac{1}{2}$ miles in six hours. Symington's reward was a general thumbs-down from the Forth and Clyde shareholders, convinced as a body that the new tug would still dangerously erode the banks of the canal. The *Charlotte Dundas* was laid up and eventually, in 1861, scrapped.

Symington's American counterpart was Robert Fulton, a failed painter-turned-engineer who spent several years at the turn of the century trying to impress first Napoleon's ministers, then their enemy counterparts in Britain, with the virtues of his *Nautilus* (1801) and other submersibles that would creep beneath the enemy's defences and demolish his surface ships and harbour installations. Both sides declared the idea a dishonourable means of waging war but could not resist allowing Fulton to hold trials. His vessels were too slow, however, and he got no further with them, not even back home in the United States. On his return there in 1806 he set about building a steamboat, which was ready in August 1807 for trials.

Steamboat, as it was first called, was 150 feet (45·7 metres) long and drove two side paddles using a Boulton and Watt single-cylinder condensing steam engine. On her first run up the Hudson River from New York to Albany, *Steamboat* covered the 150 miles in 32 hours – compared to the four days needed under sail: her noisy performance stirred one bystanding farmer to liken her to 'the Devil on a sawmill'. Renamed the *North River Steamboat*, then after a partial refit *The New North River Steamboat of Clermont*, which was shortened by the Press to *Clermont*, the paddle-steamer traded profitably on the Albany run, carrying up to 90 passengers per trip. The paddle-steamer soon caught on, and in less than 25 years some 230 steamboats were at work on America's booming river trade.

Where Symington had been disappointed Henry Bell with his *Comet* succeeded. In 1812 the $21\frac{1}{2}$-tonner became the first steamboat in Europe to run a

An early French steamboat on the river Seine in Paris.

regular passenger service, at first between Glasgow and Greenock. *Comet* and *Clermont* were the breakthrough vessels, but they of course had their limitations. They were river boats, and the next challenge was to cross the oceans under steam. *Comet*, originally only 45 feet (13·7 metres) long, was 'stretched' by 20 feet (6 metres) to help her tackle coastal trips and for a time she worked the Firth of Forth. In 1820, on a voyage between Glasgow and Fort William, she was wrecked on Craignish Point.

CHALLENGE OF THE OCEANS

Next major record-breaker was the *Savannah* (1818). Although her single-cylinder engine was little more than a modest auxiliary power source to the sails of a three-masted full-rigger, she was the first ocean-going ship capable of steam propulsion to cross the Atlantic. She made the voyage, from Savannah to Liverpool, in 1819 in 29 days and used her engine for $3\frac{1}{2}$ days on the crossing. Failing to interest prospective buyers in Europe, her owners ordered her back to Savannah, her machinery was removed and she was 'demoted' to a sailing coaster; in 1821 she was wrecked off Long Island.

The *Savannah*'s voyage was not made in vain. Time and again, the industrial originals of the 19th century were ignored in their own time, and while the businessmen retired in shock at their advent to consider what commercial mileage might be had from them, the originals were allowed to decay.

But progress was slowly made on most fronts. The year after the *Savannah* went under, the *Aaron Manby* was assembled in sections at the Surrey Commercial Docks. It was the first iron-hulled ship, also the first to be prefabricated. She was sold to a French company which used her on the Seine between Le Havre and Paris. Again, the response to a new shipbuilding method was slow, but within 20 years the value of iron ships was demonstrated – if negatively – when they showed themselves able to resist with a few dents weather that broke up wooden ships. One such was Isambard Kingdom Brunel's *Great Britain*, driven ashore at Dundrum Bay, Ireland, in 1846 and refloated a year later. That sturdy hull can still be seen today, preserved in the dry dock in Bristol where she was built.

Before looking in more detail at that extraordinary ship, we should turn back to events involving one of Brunel's earlier designs, the *Great Western* (1837), and a rival, *Sirius*, built the same year. Both Brunel and the firm of Robert Menzies, which built *Sirius*, were convinced that steam need no longer be a mere auxiliary source of power, and that a steamship could now cross the Atlantic without sails and without refuelling. In the end it was a race

The world's oldest working steamboat, Brunel's drag boat was built in 1844 to help clear the mud from Bridgwater Dock. She is now kept at Exeter Maritime Museum. In the background is the Arab pearling dhow seen in Chapter 1.

Top: I. K. Brunel's monster ship, once justly known as *Leviathan* before her name was changed to *Great Eastern*. At 18,915 tons and a length of 680 feet (208·7 metres) at the waterline, she dwarfed all other ships of her day. Seen here at the yard in Millwall, she resisted efforts to launch her for three months, eventually slipping onto the Thames on 31 January 1858.

Left: The *Great Eastern* was too big for the passenger trade available. She worked, as here, for various companies until 1865 and was then converted to lay the Atlantic Cable.

to see who could build the ship and make the crossing first. On 23 April 1838 *Sirius* arrived in New York just four hours before the *Great Western*, though in a slower overall time: 18 days 10 hours against 15 days 5 hours.

The mid-century was dominated by Brunel, a brilliant all-round engineer, founder of the Great Western Railway, builder of fine stations and bridges and a series of ships that set new standards in ocean travel. After the success of the wooden *Great Western*, the first ship capable of sustained transatlantic service, Brunel determined to build an even better ship of iron. Initially he proposed using paddle wheels for his new ship, then his attention was drawn to the rapid advances in screw propulsion.

Various names are associated with the invention of the screw propeller, one of the first being Leonardo da Vinci! After a long gap, John Stevens from New Jersey achieved partial success on a small scale with his boat *Little Juliana*, built in 1804. Then in the 1830s several men made great advances. One was John Ericsson, an adventurous marine engineer from Sweden. He patented his first screw propeller in 1836, and saw it installed the following year in the *Francis B Ogden*. He then built a small screw-powered iron ship for the US Navy which, named *Princeton*, was delivered in 1839.

The French, meanwhile, claim the honour of designing the first working screw propeller for their engineer Pierre Sauvage, who patented his invention in 1832. A little-known Bohemian, Joseph Ressels, who carried out trials at Trieste in 1829, also has his sponsors. But the feat that most impressed Brunel was that of Francis Smith with his *Archimedes* (1838), a 240-tonner which, fitted initially with a screw 7 feet (2·1 metres) in diameter, circumnavigated Britain in 1840.

33

Right: One of Brunel's many successes was the SS *Great Britain*, the first screw-powered iron ship to cross the Atlantic. Launched in 1843, she outlived by far the *Great Eastern*: even so, the first phase of her career was brief, ending after she was driven aground in Dundrum Bay, Ireland, in 1846, as shown here.

Below: In 1970 the *Great Britain* was rescued from obscurity in the Falkland Isles and towed home on a gigantic raft to her original home in Bristol, where she has been restored.

Brunel was convinced. He scrapped the paddle wheels for SS *Great Britain* and designed a steam-driven six-bladed propeller that in trials in 1844 achieved a speed of 11 knots. Eventually a four-bladed version was preferred, which vibrated less. SS *Great Britain* was the largest ship of her day. She had a gross tonnage of 3,270, was 322 feet (98 metres) long, 50 feet (15·2 metres) in the beam and could carry 360 passengers. She was also rigged – it should not be forgotten – with six masts giving a total sail area of 15,300 square feet (1,420 square metres). Her maiden voyage began on 26 July 1845, when after spending some weeks on display in London she set sail from Liverpool and arrived in New York in under 15 days.

Great Britain was a success, and would have worked the Atlantic route for many years had she not been driven aground on the Irish coast in 1846. Her strong hull survived the pounding of waves and weather for many months, until she was eventually refloated and sold by the Great Western company for service in the Australian trade. She was rerigged with three masts and ended her working life in 1886 when she took refuge in the Falkland Islands and was left to rot. In 1970 she was towed back to her home port at Bristol aboard a massive raft.

Despite Brunel's evident confidence in the screw propeller, would-be owners of screw-driven ships were cautious and held off. While they wavered, propeller enthusiasts such as Francis Smith were encouraged to take part in a new form of nautical spectacular – the tug-of-war. In 1845, Smith's *Rattler*, the Royal Navy's first screw-powered ship, was at one end of the ropes in an Admiralty-sponsored tug-of-war against the paddle-wheeler *Alecto*. The ships stood stern to stern, and at a given signal went full steam ahead. Both ships had 200-hp engines, but *Rattler*'s system of propulsion was the stronger, and the crew of *Alecto* had the humiliating experience of being towed backwards at 2·5 knots while on full power.

Another great figure of the mid-19th century was Samuel Cunard. A merchant from Halifax, Nova Scotia, Cunard expanded from small-time mail-carrier between Halifax and Boston and Bermuda to a world-wide entrepreneur. In 1838 Cunard arrived in Britain and founded the British and North American Royal Mail Steam Packet Company. His object was to start the first regular transatlantic steamship service. He proposed to employ four

Not many photographs were taken of the ill-fated *Titanic*, which sank in 1912 on her maiden voyage. She was designed to be the most luxurious ship afloat, with electric lifts, a squash court, gymnasium, and the first swimming pool installed on an Atlantic liner.

ships on the run, and when in 1839 he had procured a contract for the new service and a government subsidy, he went ahead with his first ship, the *Britannia*, with engines by Robert Napier.

Britannia was a wooden barque-rigged paddle-steamer 207 feet (63 metres) long and with a gross tonnage of 1,156. She carried a crew of 89 to sail the ship and look after 115 passengers who, if they had expected luxury, found themselves with rather less. The fine fittings of the state rooms and saloons did not mask the cramped and creaking cabins, filled with alien smells. Nor did they discourage the persistent companionship of rats, whose numbers on the early transatlantic steamers led to the ships' captains being ordered not to leave Southampton without at least one cat on board. A basic structural problem with the paddle-wheelers was that the paddles and machinery had to be placed amidships, and the passenger cabins had to be fore and aft, where they suffered more as the ship rolled and pitched. In other ways, nonetheless, Cunard demonstrated that he had the customers' best interests at heart: fresh milk, reserved for women, children and invalids, came direct from the ship's cow that lived on board. Above all, Cunard offered speed and reliability on his 'Atlantic greyhounds'. *Britannia* made her first Liverpool–Boston crossing in 14 days 8 hours, and soon her three sister ships *Arcadia*, *Caledonia* and *Columbia* were at sea. The *Andes*, Cunard's first iron screw-driven ship, joined his fleet in 1852. By this time Cunard had established that transatlantic ships could run to timetables, delivering passengers and mail at specified dates. The notion that 'the ship must get through' was so impressed on crew and public alike that, rather than leave the *Britannia* iced up in Boston, the people of that city in 1844 carved a 7-mile channel through the ice so that she could get clear. (There was an element of self-interest in the Bostonians' good deed, in that they did not wish to lose *Britannia*'s profitable business to another port; New York, in particular, was a feared rival.)

Queen of the Eastern route was the P & O company's *Himalaya*, the largest steamer in the world at her launching in 1853. She was 340 feet (103·7 metres) long with a gross tonnage of 3,438. Before the Suez Canal was opened in 1869, passengers and cargo sailed to Alexandria, then spent three uncomfortable days crossing the 250-mile-wide isthmus. As many as 3,000 camels ferried everything needed, including coal, for the second sea leg of the journey, which began at the port of Suez. The *Himalaya*, pride of the Peninsular and Oriental Steam Navigation Company, was designed for the first part of the run, from London to Alexandria.

Once the Suez Canal was open, the journeys to and from British India were affairs of comparative luxury, with spacious deck rooms, perhaps a music room, heavy buttoned leather chairs everywhere and mahogany fittings, each ventilated by a punkah. This was a piece of cloth suspended on a frame from the ceiling; with a servant to agitate the cord controls, refreshing breaths of air swept this way and that above the passengers' perspiring brows. Many of the new iron ships were built with the first-class trade very much in mind. The P & O, for example, did not take third-class passengers or emigrants, and the proportion of first to second-class passengers was weighted as far as possible in favour of the former. The P & O's luxurious steamer *Rome*, built in 1881, took 160 first-class and 60 second-class passengers. For maximum comfort, the very rich could opt for the shelter afforded by the posh cabins. This was the origin of the word, and it stood for 'Port Outward Starboard Home'.

To return to the 1850s, decade of the *Himalaya*, two other important events should be noted. One is technical, the other is the *Great Eastern*. The technical landmark was the improved compound engine, which scientists and engineers had been working on for 70 or more years. Their aim was to build an engine with a greater working output than the simple one-cylinder, little changed since James Watt had invented it. John Elder, a Scot, in 1854 came up with an engine in which the steam in one cylinder drove a piston, and was

The Cunard liner *Mauretania* at sea. She captured the Blue Riband for the fastest Atlantic crossing in 1907 (27·4 knots) and held it until 1929.

One of the greatest of the ocean queens, the *Mauretania* was the first liner to be powered by steam turbines.

then passed into a second, larger cylinder where its expansion was enough to drive a second piston. Elder's engine was successfully installed in a ship called the *Brandon*, and further advances in the use of steel instead of iron and in better designs for boilers soon followed, with the result that by 1870 ships were able to steam much greater distances without refuelling.

Brunel hatched his plan for a monster ship in an appropriate year, 1851, when Britain was swelled with pride by the Great Exhibition in Hyde Park. She would be big enough to carry 4,000 passengers, or up to 10,000 troops in an emergency, and with space for 12,000 tons of coal she would be able to sail round the world without a fuel stop. Originally named *Leviathan*, she was twice the length of the *Himalaya* and had nearly six times that ship's tonnage. At the waterline, *Leviathan* was 680 feet (208·7 metres) long, in the beam she was 82 feet 6 inches (25·1 metres) or 118 feet (35·9 metres) including the paddle-boxes, and her gross tonnage was 18,915. For power she had the paddles plus a screw propeller plus sails carried on six masts.

If she proved troublesome to build, and she did, her scale being far beyond anyone's previous experience, her launching surpassed all other difficulties. When the day came – 3 November 1857 – half London poured eastwards to the Isle of Dogs to watch the spectacle. They saw the vast hull suspended in two huge, and untested, cradles above the iron slipways. At 12.30 pm Brunel, made nervous to within a degree of collapse by delays, enormous financial pressures and the knowledge that the launch gear was unproven, gave the word to knock away the wedges keeping the cradles in position. Winches, supported by two hydraulic rams, strained and whined. The crowd waited. Nothing happened. It was raining heavily when the bow cradle stuttered a few feet forward, panicking the winchmen who fled, and a spectator in the path of a flying winch handle was dismembered. The task of slipping the re-named *Great Eastern* onto the Thames was postponed.

It took three months, and numerous attempts, before she was at last floated off on 31 January 1858. The strain on Brunel, who had spent day and night at the yard, was too much. Fatally weakened, he died in September 1858 while *Great Eastern* was undergoing trials in the English Channel. On her maiden voyage the following year she carried 38 passengers. The statistic is typical of all that was wrong with her: too big for the available passenger trade, under-powered for heavy weather, she was perhaps *the* example of Victorian industrial gigantism. Various companies tried her as a passenger or cargo vessel before she was converted to lay the Atlantic Cable in 1865, and finally scrapped in 1888.

It was also during the 1850s that shipowners became convinced that iron was more economic as well as safer than wood. The growth in their profits made them favourable to the next revolution – the exchange of steel for iron. Steel was again tougher, and lighter, and was used for shipbuilding from the mid-1860s. Then came triple-expansion engines, and yet others which passed the steam through four and even five cylinders. In the face of the growing reliability of mechanical power, the need to carry sails diminished, and be-fore the end of the '80s Atlantic liners such as the White Star Line's *Majestic* dispensed with them altogether.

The Atlantic was undoubtedly the most glamorous route, linking Old Europe with New York and the fast-expanding cities of the United States. But major commercial steam routes were now spanning the world. Some, covered by such lines as the American Pacific Mail Steam-Ship Company and the Pacific Steam Navigation Company, worked the western coasts of America, and profited greatly from the California gold rush, which began in 1848. First steamship to appear in the Pacific was the former company's *California*. In the 1880s the Pacific Mail won a contract to operate a mail service between San Francisco and Yokohama and Hong Kong. Against the tide of mechanical progress the company built the *Great Republic* and three sister ships of wood and powered them with paddles, defending the choice of paddles by arguing that the amount of coal needed to cross the Pacific (some 5,000 miles wide) would have cut severely into cargo space.

The public's eye was caught less by matters of cargo space than by stories of speed and luxury, in particular on the transatlantic Blue Riband route. The Blue Riband was the prize for the fastest crossing. Though itself non-existent, until the British MP Harold Hales donated a silver trophy in the 1930s, the Blue Riband was eagerly sought for its prestige value since it was first claimed in 1840 by the Cunarder *Arcadia*. The years from then until World War I, en-compassing Victorian grandeur, Nineties frivolity and the great Edwardian autumn of privileged opulence, were the true age of the liner.

Many great vessels contested the prized Blue Riband since *Arcadia* was robbed of the title in that magnificent year of achievement, 1851, by an American liner, the Collins company ship *Pacific*, which crossed at an average speed of 13 knots. Notable achievers in the pre-war period were the German ship *Kaiser Wilhelm der Grosse*, the first to have four funnels, which managed 22·33 knots in 1897, and the *Mauretania*, which pushed up the target to 27·4 knots in 1907. The competition persisted in the inter-war years, and in 1937 the *Queen Mary* and the *Normandie* both crossed at speeds of more than 30 knots, while the definitive crossing was made in 1952 by the *United States* which set a new speed of 35·59 knots. With her the trophy passed into per-petual storage, the race to win it outpaced forever by jet air travel. The trophy is now kept at the U.S. Merchant Marine Academy at King's Point, Long Island.

Even by the turn of the century, methods of propulsion had been revo-lutionized, firstly by the steam turbines of Sir Charles Parsons. The new turbines were first fitted in Parsons's *Turbinia*, a 44-ton launch which stormed between the lines of ships at the 1897 Spithead Review at a speed of 34·5 knots. After much heart-searching among the directors of the Cunard Line, turbines were installed in 1905 in the *Mauretania* with the triumphant result mentioned above. The ship then held the Blue Riband for 22 years.

The next great technical change was the work of Rudolf Diesel. His experiments with a heavy oil-burning engine took first shape on an ocean-going ship in the cargo vessel *Selandia*, built in 1912. This and the later change to nuclear power naturally affected cargo as well as passenger ships, but our main topic in the rest of this chapter remains the great ocean-going liners in their climactic phase.

MARITIME PALACES

What was it like to set off from Europe in the late 19th or early 20th century? So far as the shipowners were concerned, heaven was the limit. Anything you could do in the world's greatest hotels, you could expect to do in the first-class accommodation of a luxury transatlantic liner. There were even some unexpected attractions, not least the pleasure of getting married in mid-ocean.

The companies produced enormous brochures full of seductive Art Nouveau curves and curlicues. That for the *Campania* (1893), the Cunard Line's first twin-screw steamer, allocated more than 100 pages to describing the splendours of the fittings and facilities, and dwelt lingeringly on the ship's thoroughly up-to-date blend of electric lighting and cosy coal fires, the otto-

A first-class dining room aboard the French liner *Normandie* (1935), which took the Blue Riband at 29·9 knots powered by electric turbines. Transatlantic travel on this exalted scale vanished with the coming of World War II, and afterwards never regained its former heights.

mans to lounge in, the organ with gilded pipes to marvel at. Nor could the same line be accused of selling its customers short in the promises surrounding the *Mauretania*. In the public rooms the decorative styles were French or Italian Renaissance; the electric lifts were clad in grilles of exquisite ironwork after a 15th-century model; the furniture styles of Adam, Sheraton and Chippendale were represented in the state-rooms; the lavatory fittings in the first-class state rooms and the royal suite were silver-plated. Later came the demand for swimming pools, and the first to be fitted, ironically, was aboard the *Titanic*, of which more later.

Below: One of the *Normandie*'s chief rivals was the British *Queen Mary*, which operated successfully after the war and then was sold as a hotel-museum to a company in Long Beach, California.

Left: The second *Mauretania*, launched in 1939 and larger than her more famous predecessor but not as fast. As a troopship in 1945 she sailed 28,000 miles in 81½ days.

First, though, we should turn to a problem that no maritime promoter
could ever totally ignore, however much he might wish it did not exist. Even
with modern drugs and stabilizers sea-sickness is not banished. Attempts to
play down its effects by delicate reference to *mal de mer* are small comfort to the
passenger in its grip.

With typical Victorian optimism the great iron and steel master Henry
Bessemer thought he had the answer. He designed a stable saloon which, suspended within the hull on gimbals, always remained level – like a compass –
however much the outer ship heaved from side to side. The same principle

had been behind Newell's oscillating couch of 1870, a stable tub attached to hangers which the passenger climbed into in his cabin. That had not worked, but *The Graphic* in 1874 was utterly enthusiastic about the prospects of Mr Bessemer's device:

'. . . the saloon, being virtually isolated from the hull of the ship and subject to the action of Mr Bessemer's hydraulic levelling apparatus, is designed to remain absolutely unaffected, no matter how much the vessel may roll. Mr Bessemer's approved statement indicates that sea-sickness among passengers is completely eliminated, all sense of pitching and rolling being so small as to be inappreciable. Mr Bessemer's hydraulic apparatus is an established certainty, and not a matter of speculation . . .'

Good old Bessemer, many must have thought at the time. The only 'established certainty', however, was that the inventor had made a scaled-down model work in his back garden, with a steam-driven donkey engine playing the part of God and the elements. But Bessemer could do little to control fore-and-aft pitch, and his 350-ton test ship, launched in 1875, and fitted with a saloon gloriously furnished in High Gin Palace style, gave neither confidence nor stability.

One way out for the shipping lines was to try and laugh off the difficulties. In 1896 the White Star Line produced a guide with jocular hints such as 'Don't go to the table unless confident of your ability to stay there'. 'If a contribution to Neptune becomes unavoidable, do not become discouraged, but continue to eat . . .' There was little to be done, indeed, but wait for technology to make the ships more stable, and this took a long time. Even aboard the spectacularly modern *Bremen*, launched in 1928, winner of the Blue Riband on her maiden voyage, the recommended cure was the Dammert Inhalation Treatment. This daunting process, invented by the ship's surgeon, Dr Dammert, involved standing on deck and inhaling a mixture of oxygen (to revive the system) and atropine (to calm the nerves).

Sea travel has always seemed to mix the sublime with the dangerous and, on occasion, the sordid. For the most part passengers have been prepared to

The *Bremen*, successor to the great Norddeutscher liner of the inter-war years.

The P & O cruise liner *Chusan* leaving Southampton. She was scrapped in the late 1970s.

accept the whole package in the hope that sublimity would dominate the other two. No better example can eclipse the story of the *Titanic*. It is all too well known how this great 'unsinkable' British liner struck an iceberg near Newfoundland on her maiden voyage in 1912 and foundered in the night with a loss of 1,513 lives. She had 14 watertight compartments and could survive even if four were flooded. The ultimate danger, it seemed, was conquered. And yet the iceberg ripped a 300-foot (90-metre) gash in her side and in two hours she was swallowed by the Arctic waters. Her sinking forced a rapid tightening of radio safety controls, greater provision of lifeboats (she had only 1,178 spaces for the 2,224 people on board) and the establishment of an International Ice Patrol to warn ships of icebergs on the North Atlantic routes.

None of what subsequently happened could reduce the optimism of her owners, the White Star Line, when she was built. She was, unquestionably, the most luxurious ship afloat, with unsurpassed facilities. Passengers were transported from deck to deck by electric lifts; there was a gymnasium with rowing machines and mechanical horses; a squash court; the first-ever swimming pool on an Atlantic liner; Turkish baths; a palm court; a *café parisien*; a grand dining-room hung with Aubusson tapestries. In short, no ocean liner had ever offered its customers more, nor so quickly had its promise withdrawn.

One of today's great liners, the *QE2*, a cruise ship of 65,864 tons. Her future, however, remains indefinite in a world where a ship with nearly 900 cabins is not everyone's choice for a luxury holiday.

Longest liner in the world, the *France* was built in 1961 for the New York run. The wings on the funnels are designed to divert flying dirt specks from the passenger decks.

The sinking of the *Titanic* prompted public doubt over the wisdom of building so massive a ship. Yet soon the German Hamburg-Amerika Line had three still larger vessels afloat – the *Imperator*, *Vaterland* and *Bismarck*. The lure of the Atlantic was far from dead, and in the inter-war years many more fine ships came into service. While the German *Bremen* (1928), the French *Normandie* (1935) and the British *Queen Mary* (1936) vied on the Atlantic route for the custom of the famous and the attention of mass newspaper readerships, in the Pacific the *Empress of Japan* (1930) became the largest and most luxurious liner to ply between Vancouver and Hong Kong, putting in also at Victoria, Honolulu and Yokohama. By then steam turbines were not the only means of propulsion. Electric turbines powered the *Normandie*, for example, and the world was by then on the brink of discovering nuclear power.

The nuclear revolution has not so far dominated the luxury liner. Sheer cost has prevented this, and operating costs have changed the role of the liner, too. Today's great ships, the *QE2* (1968), the *Hamburg* (1969) and others less grand are built more for pleasure cruising than for running on regular ocean services. In terms of comfort they have much to offer, though it is more the homogenized variety of the American hotel chain. The great romance, fatally diluted, is all but over. Queens of the '30s are museums today, or dead. The *Queen Mary* is a kitsch hotel-museum in Long Beach, California. Her sister ship, *Queen Elizabeth*, built in 1938, was sold to owners in Florida to become a convention centre. When that venture collapsed, she was bought by a Hong Kong businessman, renamed *Seawise University*, and sailed on her last voyage to Hong Kong, where in January 1972 she caught fire and toppled onto the harbour bed.

Of their three great successors, two are out of service, the *United States* and the *France*, while the *QE2* is a pale example of her forebears, a floating hotel whose destination no longer matters. Nostalgia for passenger steam at sea would probably be as great as the current passion for putting steam back on the railways. Unfortunately, when the object of one's affection is about 1,000 feet long and weighs 50,000 tons, it may be wiser to stick to models and dreams of bygone luxury. Or divert one's feelings to something a little smaller; a steam launch or tug, perhaps. A few still remain, lovingly preserved by such organizations as the Maritime Trust in London's St. Katharine's Dock, the Exeter Maritime Museum and the Windermere Steamboat Museum.

Probably the fastest passenger liner there will ever be – the *United States*, which took the Blue Riband in 1952 at 34·5 knots. Jet air travel has outpaced the need for more such performances at sea.

Typical of the modern cruise ship is the *Starward*, a sea-going hotel in all but name, here pictured in the West Indies.

Fighting Ships

GALLEYS AND GALLEASSES

The role of the fighting ship has changed surprisingly little since the combined Greek fleet routed the Persians and their allies at Salamis in 480 B.C. in one of the best-documented early naval battles. The Greek oared galleys were, in essence, platforms for combat at sea. Up to 40 helmeted men-at-arms, the equivalent of marines, and archers occupied a narrow fighting bridge running from stem to stern. From there they showered the enemy with arrows and, at close-quarters, javelins. Motive power came from the oarsmen, their oars ranged in banks of three in the triremes and two in the biremes. The other offensive weapon was a bronze ram or beak attached to the prow. Under the skilful guidance of the helmsmen, the beak could dash against the side of an enemy ship, ripping a hole beneath the waterline. If the enemy did not sink when rival ships clashed, the men-at-arms led a boarding charge. The Persians, unlike the Greeks, were poor swimmers, and at Salamis it was enough for the Greeks to tip their foe overboard to eliminate them. Soon, as Aeschylus graphically wrote in *The Persians*:

'Crushed hulls lay upturned on the sea so thick
You could not see the water, choked with wrecks
And slaughtered men; while all the shores and reefs
Were strewn with corpses. Soon in wild disorder
All that was left of our fleet turned tail and fled.'

The Battle of Salamis is important in naval history because its outcome turned entirely on events at sea. The land armies took virtually no part, and the stock of the Greek sailors soared from 'naval rabble' to Athens' splendid and glorious navy. Major battles at sea, fought independently of land support, were rare in Antiquity. Most encounters took the form of naval raids to gain by force goods not available through the peaceful channels of trade. Early sailors from Egypt preferred, moreover, to stay inshore in their flimsy ships of pegged acacia blocks, and this tradition survived even when their shipbuilders had supplies of Phoenician cedar to work with, which gave them longer and stronger planks for the hulls.

A relief at Medinet Habu near Thebes, carried out in the time of Rameses III (1198–66 B.C.), shows an early naval battle in clear detail. It took place near the Nile Delta, where the Egyptian fleet succeeded in pinning their foe (broadly referred to as the Sea Peoples and probably including Cretans and the Biblical Philistines) between their vessels and the shore. Egyptian archers on land poured their fire onto the enemy, while more archers and javelin throwers aboard the Egyptian ships made it impossible for the Sea Peoples to defend themselves adequately with their round shields or to return the fire. Both navies are shown aboard sailing ships, but those of the Sea Peoples lack oars; possibly their inferior manoeuvrability had led them into the trap. An interesting feature of the Egyptian ships is a 'top' or crow's nest above the yard, manned by a slinger.

In Classical times the biremes and triremes were given such refinements as leather tarpaulins rolled down over the rowing compartments to protect the oarsmen during battle, but the method of fighting remained much the same, and would do so until the advent of reliable cannon made it possible to fight at greater ranges and to destroy the enemy by sinking his ship from a distance as an alternative to overcoming him in hand-to-hand combat.

The Byzantines, whose capital was Constantinople (Istanbul), improved and enlarged the oared warship. Their chief type was the dromon, and by the 12th century A.D. it was worked by 200–300 men who pulled two banks of oars on either side of the ship. There was greater reliance on sail, and the ram was raised above the waterline. The Byzantines also added to the range of weapons with their 'Greek fire', a primitive flamethrower that launched in-

Above: Christians and Turks do violent battle at Lepanto in 1571. This was the last major clash of oar-powered warships.

Right: Centuries before Lepanto, the Viking design for long narrow warships was followed by the Anglo-Saxons and Normans. This segment of the Bayeux Tapestry shows how a longship of the late 11th century was sailed and steered.

flammable liquid through a bronze tube. On touching water, the liquid ignited. Also carried on the medieval dromons were versions of the ballista, a high-powered crossbow modified to fire javelins at a much greater velocity than the human arm could achieve; stone balls could also be fired using a naval version of the siege catapult.

The next step along this line of development, which was essentially Mediterranean, was the galleass. The lateen rig was long established when in the early 16th century ships appeared which relied for manoeuvrability on a smaller number of oars each pulled by about five men. The galleasses usually carried a single but large lateen-rigged mast, and they were armed with cannon – as many as the ship would carry. The concept of sets of broadside guns was some years away, and the guns were emplaced in fixed positions in fore and after-castles, or pivoted from swivels on the open deck. The heaviest gun, a kind of bombard, fired forward over the beak.

At the height of their development, in 1571, galleys and galleasses fought a stirring engagement at Lepanto. Compared with paintings of the Battle of the Armada, fought in stand-off style 17 years later, Lepanto *looks* more exciting because of the extraordinarily tight press of ships. Jammed chaotically together at all angles, Christians and Turks blast each other with bombards,

The British fireships seek out victims among the Spanish Armada. The main effect of this battle was to affirm the arrival of the gunned battleship firing broadsides of heavy cannon. After 1588 no major sea power could think of arming its battle fleet otherwise.

lighter-weight demi-culverins and sakers, and handguns. On one ship, shortly to join the fight at close range, infantry formed in a block around the mast emphasize that ramming and boarding were still the essential means of victory. The guns were useful as weapons of terror, but as yet they were not battle-winners.

In the Mediterranean these beliefs persisted until the 18th century, long after the Northern full-rigged ships and the galleons had shown the shattering superiority of the windship armed with broadsides of cannon. The main reason for their persistence seems to have been that no ruler with a Mediterranean seaboard to defend was prepared to sacrifice the manoeuvrability granted by oars in a sea where the winds were usually light. And for as long as the chief system of propulsion – the oarsmen – occupied the middle of the ship, no broadsides of cannon could be mounted in that space. In the end, without growing to dinosaur proportions to prove the point, the galleass demonstrated an impossible equation. The more guns it carried, the heavier it became, and less manoeuvrable, so needing more oarsmen when the ideal was to have fewer. The French réale was an interesting survivor, as were the Corsair galleys, but the world had grown larger and the balance of sea power was now contested elsewhere.

The narrow fighting ships of the Vikings, the drakkars, were untypical of the way warships later took shape in the North Sea and Atlantic. Although undoubtedly long, up to 150 feet (45·7 metres), they were also spacious, and were rowed by up to 80 men, 40 on each side, the oars being fitted through holes in the ship's sides. The immediate descendants of the drakkars were the Norman longships used in 1066 by William the Conqueror to gain a foothold on England's south coast. As we know from the Bayeux Tapestry, made in the 11th century, the longships were broad enough to carry an army complete with horses and stores.

But by the time Richard I was setting off on the Third Crusade in the late 12th century, military transport was provided by round ships. Indeed there was little difference between military and cargo ships in those days. The farther men travelled, the wiser they would be to go well armed, and in battle pictures of the 14th and 15th century the ships of northern Europe bristle with spears and bows jutting from the fore- and aftercastles and the sometimes dangerously overloaded fighting tops.

Sail had passed into the age of the carrack, and the full-rigged ship was at hand. The 'kraek' of the Flemish master 'W.A.' is a heavily armed trader, but it could have been manned for battle. In the original drawing from which our knowledge is derived, the three 'tops' show a variety of arms including a swivel gun on the mizzen, and on the port side of the aftercastle the muzzles of five cannon are visible.

The next step was to extend the high aftercastle forward, producing more space for rows of cannon. By contrast with Henry V's *Grâce à Dieu*, started in 1416 and armed with only three guns, the big ships of Henry VII – *Regent* and *Sovereign*, both of 1488 – had a vast complement of guns, 225 and 141 respectively. Admittedly, these were mostly iron 'serpentnes' of small calibre, firing 'pellettes of lede', and each ship also relied heavily on some 200 bowmen.

The Portuguese under King John II were also making great strides. Their caravels were not large, and had about 20 bombards apiece, but Vasco da Gama in 1501 skilfully deployed his fleet, outnumbered at least 4 to 1 by the 'ships of Mecca' – mostly ocean-going dhows with smaller support ships – off the Malabar coast of India, and destroyed the enemy. The Moors also had artillery, but these were smaller pieces, many of the lobbing mortar type, and the Portuguese easily outranged them. This was the key to their success, and the Malabar battle may be the first stand-off naval battle in history. No attempt was made to board the enemy vessels. Instead, by guns alone they were 'much ill-treated', wrote the Portuguese chronicler Gaspar Correar, 'they were broken and stove in, and many had the masts and yards shattered, which was the greatest advantage our men obtained.'

Now was the time of the prestige ship, with which to dazzle rival nations. Henry VIII rebuilt his father's *Sovereign* and added two more, the *Mary Rose*

In this painting by Nicholas Pocock of the Battle of the Nile (1798), Nelson's leading ships aim to round and infiltrate the van of the French line, anchored across Aboukir Bay, and so snare the enemy in a deadly crossfire.

(1513) and the *Henry Grâce à Dieu* or 'Great Harry' (1514). His shipwrights pioneered the hull gun port, cut in the sides of the ships at different deck levels, which made for a more even distribution of weight. The cast bronze long-gun offered better ranges; being muzzle-loading, it could take a higher charge load than the dangerous breech-loaders with their detachable chambers which were prone to explode in the gunner's face. Muzzle-loaders took longer to load, however, and left their crews exposed to enemy fire in the intervals. The ideal gun-type was the breech-loader, but the search for effective versions was to last for more than 300 years.

Before the galleon with its broadsides of guns entered service in the 1580s, most sea fights were still contested by the old boarding tactics. These were, admittedly, a last resort, but in practice the artillery was not powerful enough to shatter the stout wooden planks of a North European enemy at long range (as distinct from the Arab dhows which da Gama easily 'stove in'). So the

ships closed, and the lighter artillery pieces were used. Then, as a Spanish naval treatise of *c.* 1530 explained, '. . . so soon as they come to board or grapple all other kinds of arms shall be used . . . more particularly first missiles, such as harpoons and stones, handguns and crossbows, and then the fireballs aforesaid . . . and at the same time the calthrops [spiked iron balls], stinkballs, grenades and scorpions for the sails and rigging.' It was vigorously organized, but it wasn't the stuff of the stand-off sea fight.

The Spanish Armada campaign of 1588 was the turning point. Although the guns of the high Spanish galleons under the command of the Duke of Medina Sidonia were much more numerous than those that Lord Howard could assemble for the English, they were of hugely varying types and capacities. And where the galleons verged dangerously on the cumbersome, the English ships, thanks to the earlier foresight of Sir John Hawkins, were lower, longer and more nimble – and so able to stay out of range of the heaviest Spanish guns. In the end, of course, it was the stratagem of the fireships which broke the Armada. But from that time no Northern country could envisage taking on an enemy fleet unless it had adequate numbers of full-rigged ships capable of delivering powerful broadsides.

Between the ages of Drake and Nelson – some 200 years – development of the fighting ship was slow. In common with the armed merchantmen, the high forecastle was shed for a lower beak-head. Guns grew bigger and more

The Dutch and British fought many a hard sea fight in the mid-17th century. Here the painter Gerard Soest portrays the Dutch fleet under Admiral de Ruyter advancing up the River Medway in 1667.

numerous, and the space for them increased. Allowance was made for recoil and it became regular practice to haul in the guns after firing, reload and run the muzzles out again through the gun ports. This was a great improvement on the earlier practice – probably never universal but widely used – of loading outboard, with a gunner perched on top of the muzzle while the sponges, rammers and balls, were passed out to him. It must have been highly dangerous for the men during battle – although in Elizabethan times the tactic of firing one broadside, then tacking away from the enemy before returning to hit him with the other side, would have given the gunners reasonable time to do their work while facing away from the enemy's fire.

The method of fighting with ships in line ahead may have been used as early as 1639 by the Dutch Admiral van Tromp. With modification, it survived to the Napoleonic Wars, by which time it was common for opposing ships to blast each other from point-blank range until one ship and/or its crew were fatally weakened.

Attrition was accepted as an essential ingredient of victory no matter how ingenious the commanders were in achieving tactical superiority. One of Rear-Admiral Horatio Nelson's most glorious victories, in the Battle of the Nile, was not won without sustained pounding from both sides.

It was 1800 hours, with only two hours of daylight remaining on 1 August 1798 when Nelson's lookouts at last spotted the French battle fleet of Admiral Brueys at anchor across the face of Aboukir Bay. Brueys had mounted shore batteries to cover his flanks, but their fire could not prevent the five leading British ships from slipping past the van of the French line. As they began their attack on the inshore side, Nelson in *Vanguard* sailed with his 10 remaining ships along the French line on the seaward side. Each British captain was ordered to 'feel' for an opponent in the gathering darkness, and they opened a ferocious double-sided fire. Brueys had 13 ships caught in the sandwich, and they responded nobly. The French flagship *L'Orient* had 120 guns and this devastating firepower shattered the 74-gun *Bellerophon*. The British line persisted, and *L'Orient* then was attacked on both quarters by *Swiftsure* and *Alexander*. The guns roared in the darkness, masts and rigging toppled in the confused inferno around the French flagship. Brueys was cut in two by a British cannonball, but *L'Orient* fought on until the fatal blow struck and she exploded. It was then 2200 hours. Through the night the British kept up a terrible fire and when at dawn Admiral Villeneuve escaped he had only two ships of the line and two frigates left. It was a supreme victory, but it was won only after awesome bloodshed.

The weight of shot was considerably increased at the beginning of the Industrial Revolution by the invention of the carronade, named after the Carron Ironworks in Scotland where it was made. Carronades capable of firing a 32-pound (14·5-kg) ball were only 4 feet (1·2 metres) long; a cannon

Union troops in 1862 watch the battle in Hampton Roads between the Confederate ironclad *Merrimac* (later renamed *Virginia*) and the revolutionary *Monitor*, a 'cheesebox on a raft'. This first-ever fight between ironclads was inconclusive after four hours, but introduced the world to a new form of warfare at sea.

of similar length could fire only a 3-pound (1·3-kg) ball. For close-range work it was the best gun in service. The secret of its exceptional power lay in greatly reducing the windage or gap between ball and bore; much more of the energy imparted by the charge stayed behind the ball as it left the barrel instead of leaking away round the sides and being wasted. For long-range work, however, the carronade was ineffective compared with long 18- and 24-pounder cannon, and more than one admiral in the early 19th century rued his decision to convert to an all-carronade armament.

THE STEAM AND IRON GENERATIONS

After several centuries of relative calm in warship design, there were suddenly to be tremendous changes that would upset the global balance forever. One of the first men to break down the old ways was Robert Fulton, designer of the paddle-steamer *Clermont* (1807). The American War of 1812 stimulated the US government, then Fulton, to harness steam to warlike ends. He designed a double-keeled paddle-driven ship, the *Demologos*, which was eventually launched in 1814, too late for action.

Other experiments with steam were for the time being more modest. The

Later in the 19th century mines, torpedoes and primitive submarines brought further hazards to naval conflict. Here a Japanese warship approaches the mines ringing the Russian defences at Port Arthur in 1904.

British Admiralty first dipped its toe in these uncharted waters with a tug, *Monkey* (1821), whose task was to tow the sailing ships out to sea when the wind was unfavourable. Paddle-steamers were seen to be too vulnerable for combat, and the machinery too bulky at the cost of gun room.

It took many years of argument for the Admiralty to accept that steam had a future in its fighting navy. In 1828, more than a quarter of a century after the first trials of the *Charlotte Dundas*, the Admiralty still clung to its faith in sail, even for support vessels in the minor role of coastal defence. Lord Melville, then First Sea Lord, was crushing in his antagonism to steam, stating on one occasion that: 'Their Lordships feel it their bounden duty to discourage to the utmost of their ability the employment of steam vessels, as they consider that the introduction of steam is calculated to strike a fatal blow at the naval supremacy of the Empire.'

The screw propeller was an altogether better proposition, and the first nation to try it in a battleship was France; the *Napoleon* was laid down in 1850. In the meantime the Battle of Navarino Bay (1827) had gone down in history as the last battle fought entirely under sail.

Further advances in gunnery produced the cylindrical shell, with its greater hitting power – and greater accuracy imparted by the spin of rifled gun barrels. Wooden warships began to retreat behind screens of iron plating; this first phase of adaptation culminated in the French iron-protected frigate *La Gloire* (1858).

Then came HMS *Warrior* (1860), the world's first iron warship. *Warrior*'s all-metal hull posed a new problem not encountered by the first generation of iron merchantmen. As a warship *Warrior* and its immediate successors were no more than half successful, since they lacked a weapon capable of destroying another ironclad warship. The eternal duel between the defensive and the offensive had swung heavily in favour of the defensive.

In the American Civil War (1861–65) the Swedish engineer John Ericsson, who had been one of the pioneers of screw propulsion, offered the Federal

government his revolutionary design for *Monitor*, a single-turreted ship armed with two 11-inch (27·9-cm) guns. Built in 100 days, this extraordinary low-hulled vessel, more like a primitive submarine to the modern eye, fought the Confederate ironclad *Merrimac* in a six-hour battle. It was a drawn fight, but many observers were impressed with the new concept, which Ericsson had first shown to Napoleon III as far back as 1854. It marked the end of the broadside-armed ship in favour of an ironclad whose guns were protected while they swung through a wider arc of fire.

This line of thinking led to the central-battery ship, then to the turret ship. The ill-fated *Captain*, with its monstrous masts, demonstrated not only the central battery but also the folly of persisting with sail. After her it was rare for steam to be only the auxiliary and not the principal means of propulsion.

The 1860s were a confusing time in warship development. For a short while it was thought that the ineffective fire-power of the new ironclads could be helped by bringing back the ancient ram. The *Merrimac*, mentioned above, had a ram, but far greater damage – which sent many naval thinkers into a cul-de-sac for several years – was caused by Admiral Tegethoff, the Austrian commander at the Battle of Lissa (1866), who ordered his black-painted ships to 'ram everything grey'. The Austrians' grey-hulled Italian opponents were just as enthusiastic about ramming, and there were many failed attempts and near-misses before Tegethoff aboard the *Ferdinand Max* rammed and sank the already disabled Italian frigate *Re d'Italia*.

Rams were one of the shorter-lived fads of warship history. Once it was seen how easily they could be avoided, and fired on from deadly ranges, governments stopped building them. The next serious development was the monster gun, first installed in the Italian ship *Duilio* (1872) which was laid down with four 12-inch (30·4-cm) guns each weighing 38 tons. So rapidly, in fact, were the Italians convinced that they had found a battle-winner, they modified the *Duilio* twice during construction and she ended up with 17·7-inch (45-cm) guns weighing 100 tons. By their vast weight these guns posed further problems, and it was the advances of the 1880s that were to prove more important. This decade saw the introduction – at last – of efficient and lighter-weight breech-loading guns, and the Quick-Firing (QF) gun – at first as a secondary armament, but soon part of the heavy-gun battery.

The gun-armour race between the major maritime powers went steadily on. Meanwhile the undersea war had been growing in importance since the American Civil War, when a Confederate hand-cranked submerged craft had sunk the Federal sloop *Housatonic* with a torpedo carried on a spar. Other forms of torpedo were towed by wire onto the target by fast surface craft, and then after a series of trials and minor catastrophes the self-propelling locomotive torpedo entered the battleground. By the early 1890s locomotive torpedoes with a 300-pound (136-kg) warhead could be launched below the waterline of a moving ship and travel more than 1,000 yards at 30 knots. These advances spawned a new range of ship types: fast torpedo boats to launch the weapon, 'catchers' to chase and eliminate them (the first destroyers), and torpedo-armed submarines to close with their prey without being detected.

The torpedo menace was matched by the improved steel armour which clad battleships from the 1890s, and by longer-range guns capable of sinking the enemy beyond torpedo range. The grouping of the main armament in the capital ships was subject to constant experiment, and took a revolutionary turn in the *Dreadnought* of 1905. The name of this British ship became a universal term, and her system of armament was taken up by all the big powers. What was new about the *Dreadnought* was that she used a uniform set of big guns in her main armament; the ten 12-inch (30·4-cm) guns were grouped in five twin turrets, and were supported by 27 12-pounders (5·4 kg) and five 18-inch (45·7-cm) torpedo tubes. This was a far cry from the mixed collections of less powerful guns used in the battleships of the late 19th century. Navies now had the means of outranging the torpedo – by then capable of destruction at 4,000 yards – and of knocking out battleships of lesser calibre.

In the years leading up to World War I more ship types came into service. Next in size to the battleship was the battlecruiser – a heavily armed ship with the speed of a cruiser; the armoured cruiser, designed to withstand heavy fire and also fight the older battleships, and the light cruiser intended for reconnaissance. While in a sense these ships corresponded to the former British system of rating ships (1st to 6th) according to the number of guns carried, an important difference was that battles were no longer fought in line ahead; ships tended increasingly to take on individual roles – though in the 1900s these were not wholly clear, except in relation to the ships that rival powers were building. One factor felt by all powers was the sheer cost of building a modern navy, and this exerted a brake on the size and composition of battle fleets.

AGE OF THE CARRIER

One week before the outbreak of war in 1914 a Short floatplane of the newly formed Royal Naval Air Service made the first launch of an aerial torpedo. In terms of naval warfare this was a much more exciting development than the looming presence over water of the airship. Most successful of the airships was the German rigid version known as the Zeppelin after its inventor Count Ferdinand von Zeppelin, intended for bombing and reconnaissance work.

A first step in the evolution of the flight deck: a Sopwith 1½ Strutter takes off from a precarious platform mounted over a gun turret.

But the possibilities of the aircraft – additionally capable of close-range attack, using the decks of ships for landing and taking off – were to eclipse all other developments. Although their roles were hotly disputed in 1914–18, aircraft were to transform the balance of the world's navies. There is not space here to detail how the naval aircraft won its ascendancy in the coming decades, but it is safe to say that, with the submarine, it dictated the way future wars would be fought.

The techniques of flying on and off the heaving deck of a ship were still highly experimental. First man to take off from a ship was an American, Lieutenant Eugene Ely. On 14 November 1910 he flew his wheeled Curtiss biplane from a special 80-foot (24·3-metre) platform erected over the bows of the cruiser USS *Birmingham*. On 18 January the following year Ely made the first on-deck landing, alighting on the USS *Pennsylvania*. During the war British pilots gradually mastered the dangerous art of being launched by catapult from platforms mounted over the ship's guns, but the more common method was to use floatplanes which were lowered by winch on to the sea, returning by the same procedure in reverse. Not until 2 August 1917 did a British pilot, Squadron-Commander Dunning, achieve a deck landing, and three days later he was killed making a similar attempt.

Right: HMS *Ark Royal*, Britain's last big carrier, completed in 1955 with an angled flight deck to make landing safer.

Above: Carrier fighters on the flight deck of HMS *Formidable* during the North African landings of November 1942.

Left: Last of the mighty: with her sister-ship *Musashi* the largest battleship ever built, the Japanese *Yamato*, a monster of 64,000 tons, is shown being fitted out at Kure naval base in 1941. She was sunk in April 1945 by U.S. carrier-borne aircraft.

This page:
Submarine activity
around the depot
ship HMS *Forth* in
June 1943. A
21-inch (53·4-cm)
torpedo is being
swung out to a
waiting submarine of
the 3rd Flotilla.

HMS *Furious* was the ship concerned. She was a converted battlecruiser, and at first her flight-deck was fitted over the fore-deck. After the fatal accident a longer flight-deck was built aft of the bridge and funnel, and aircraft equipped with skid undercarriages performed hazardous landings made still more dangerous by the turbulent draughts from the funnels. Eventually *Furious* was refitted with a full-length flying-deck which wheeled planes could use for take-off and landing. In October 1917 converted Camels took off from *Furious* and successfully raided and burned down Zeppelin sheds at Tondern. It was a heroic mission, but somewhat ahead of its time. The first 'true' carrier, HMS *Argus*, was not completed until September 1918 – too late to see action.

HMS *Belfast*, Britain's last conventional cruiser with 6-inch (152-mm) guns, now a floating museum in the Pool of London.

The Porpoise class submarine HMS *Finwhale*, on exercise in 1976. Launched in 1959, she carries eight 21-inch (53·4-cm) torpedo tubes and is powered by diesel-electric engines — now eclipsed in potential by the nuclear generation of submarines.

Few major surface actions were contested in World War I. With the German High Seas Fleet largely ensnared by minefields in the North Sea, the Allies were content to preserve the status quo. The chief exception was the Battle of Jutland (1916), in which natural caution overrode the opportunies to gain a clinching victory. Even though, as Churchill claimed, Admiral Jellicoe was 'the only man on either side who could lose the war in an afternoon', the British commander would have had to suffer disastrous losses to bring this about. In the event the British did lose more ships than the Germans, but recovered from the initial drubbing of their battlecruisers to force the main German fleet back to their home ports, where for the most part they remained until Germany's capitulation.

In the inter-war years treaty limitations held back for a while the growth of the world's navies, until German and Japanese militarism made it clear that a new race for sea power was inevitable. In the new building programmes the battleship was still supreme; to guard against aerial and torpedo attacks, deck and hull armour were thickened, anti-aircraft guns installed, and hangar space made for carrying a small number of planes which could be launched by catapult. Meanwhile aircraft carriers of mounting capacity were being built. Although Britain in 1939 had more carriers in service than any other nation, Japan and the United States – looking respectively to further and protect their interests in the Pacific – were building much larger carriers and experimenting more adventurously with specialized aircraft – with fighters, dive-bombers and torpedo-bombers.

World War II witnessed the virtual end of the gunned battleship. In February 1942 the Japanese brought into service the biggest battleship ever built. The careers of *Yamato* and her sister ship *Musashi* were undistinguished, but their specifications were astonishing. *Yamato* displaced 64,000 tons; she was 863 feet (263 metres) long, with a beam of 127 feet (38·6 metres), and in her final armament she had nine 18-inch guns, a mass of secondary guns, 146 anti-aircraft guns and six aircraft. However, when she was caught on 7 April 1945 by US carrier planes she was powerless against their onslaught. In the space of two hours she was hit by at least seven bombs and up to 12 torpedoes aimed chiefly at her port side. At about 1430 hours she blew up in a great pillar of black-brown smoke and sank.

The naval gun platform had changed into a virtually non-combatant weapon-carrier. The mother ship remained remote from the enemy, dispatching clouds of warplanes on round-trips of several hundred miles to destroy his battle fleet. For her own defence she carried mainly anti-aircraft weapons, but relied more on her planes for protection. In the decisive Battle of the Philippine Sea, fought in June 1944, the US Admiral Spruance had 891 carrier aircraft at his disposal. His Fast Carrier Task Force contained 15 carriers, 7 battleships, 20 cruisers and 67 destroyers. Thanks to accurate radio fixes, the Americans knew where the two attacking Japanese fleets were, and were ready for them. The Japanese carrier planes were almost eliminated, only 30 surviving out of an initial strength of 430, and three carriers were sunk. The battle drew the teeth of the Imperial Japanese Navy, whose replacement rate was weak compared to that of the United States, already emerging as one of the two principal Superpowers of the post-war world.

Since World War II the thinking of the United States, the USSR and their allies, satellites and clients has been dominated by two principal factors: the

A French destroyer at the 1978 Silver Jubilee Review at Spithead.

Right: A warship of our times: the small but versatile Soviet carrier *Kiev*, equipped with anti-submarine helicopters and vertical take-off fighters.

Right: A Polaris missile breaks into the atmosphere after its launch from a submerged submarine.

Above: A new – and more economic – launch system for a new weapon: a Royal Navy patrol hydrofoil is paired with the Harpoon anti-shipping missile.

nuclear missile and the means of delivering it. In 1960 the USS *George Washington* became the first submarine to fire a missile from beneath the surface of the sea. Nuclear power was also applied to propulsion systems, although the prohibitive cost has confined this development largely to submarines. The USSR has steadily built up a vast navy of conventional ships and nuclear submarines. Outmatched by the Americans' great carrier strength, the Russians at first did not seek to compete at this level. However, they now have in ships of the *Kiev* class a type that may predominate in the years ahead: a small, fast carrier, fitted with sonar and an expensive array of long- and short-range missiles. In addition to her gun and missile equipment she can carry 20 fixed V/STOL (Vertical/Short Take Off and Landing) aircraft or 25 helicopters of the 'Hormone' type (this being their NATO codename).

The Superpowers are delicately balanced. The Americans are superior in carriers, but the Russians have a formidable force of cruisers, destroyers and submarines armed with nuclear missiles. In war, the burden would be on the Americans to deal effectively with this armada of missiles before they themselves struck. A daunting prospect, but not less so than the fact that a nuclear warship need no longer leave its home port to strike a massive blow at the enemy. Both sides are more than adequately equipped for overkill.

Special-Purpose Ships

GROWTH OF THE TANKER

Everyone knows what an oil tanker looks like. They have been one of the biggest growth areas in modern shipping. While their advent was gradual, by 1939 they made up 17 per cent of the world's merchant tonnage. At the heart of this success story was the booming motor industry, which suddenly could not get enough fuel to feed customer demand. Added to which, the world's navies from 1912 had begun to switch from coal-fired boilers into oil.

The relationship between the latest supertankers, gargantuan in length and beam with cargo capacities of 500,000 tons, and their modest ancestors is not immediately clear. On a comparison of photographs, the archetypal tanker *Glückauf*, of 1886, appears long but her decks support a clutter of superstructure including three masts. A closer look reveals the essential characteristics of the oiler: forward is a long open deck while the engines and accommodation are placed aft, with the funnel three-quarters of the way towards the stern. Below, her cargo was carried in hull compartments, not the customary barrels, and this bulk method allowed her to unload in 12 hours. Some owners were sceptical, believing the combination of 'loose' oil in a

Above: Biggest boom in post-war shipping has been the growth in numbers and individual size of the oil tankers. This vessel is BP's *British Patience*.

Left: The Esso supertanker *Skandia* off Dover. With their massive dimensions and alarmingly long stopping times, the big tankers are a particular hazard in crowded shipping lanes like the English Channel.

Right: This unusual view across the starboard bow of the supertanker *British Respect* conveys some impression of the vast capacity of the tanks in the hull.

Above: Though by the standards of most of western Europe a poor country, Greece has a huge merchant fleet. This Onassis-owned supertanker is the *Olympic Aspiration*.

steam-driven ship to be fatal. Twenty years after *Glückauf* was launched, there had been almost a complete turnround. *Glückauf* had worked, and the owners hastened to discard barrels for bulk.

The fear that tankers must have a maximum length, beyond which their backs would break, has preoccupied marine engineers and their mercantile overlords since the early 1900s. The three-islander, comprising a long hull with high forecastle, bridge amidships and aft decks, became the most popular compromise, but the insatiable demand for oil has forced dramatic expansion on the tanker, producing the familiar improbably long aft-high silhouette on horizons from Holland to Japan. Occasionally their backs do break, and the consequent inshore devastation to birds, fish, farm livestock and crops, and to the local environment as a whole rightly arouses a mountain of social protest. Are tankers too big for safety? Structurally they appear sound, but their slowed performance in turning and stopping suggests that an optimum point is near. A further limiting factor is the supertanker's reliance on massive deep-water terminals. Most harbours are dredged to depths up to

50 feet (15·2 metres) but the supertanker with a loaded draught of 80 feet (24·3 metres) and more must have special – and very expensive – port facilities.

Some tankers double as bulk-ore carriers, and are designed to take either type of cargo. Specialist bulk carriers are built to carry specific cargoes of sugar, molasses, cement, bauxite, wine, and many other dry and wet goods. Liquids have posed particular problems since some react unfavourably with the material of the container and so special linings have been evolved : of stainless steel for wine, nickel for glycerin, and so on. Temperature control is also of vital importance, and advanced technology has now made it possible for modified tankers to carry hot cargoes such as liquid sulphur in insulated steam-heated tanks kept at a constant temperature of 130°C. On arrival at the destination port, the sulphur is piped directly into heated storage tanks on land. At the opposite end of the thermometer, refrigerated cargo ships (reefers) of varying size can carry loads of tropical fruit or meat across the world in specially lined containers.

Many bulk carriers share the basic configuration of the oil tanker, and show a long low profile with engines aft. In some, however, such as the Great Lakes ships, the bridge is positioned at the forecastle. Deck gear may include grabs for unloading a cargo such as sugar, or there may be none since the necessary cranes, grabs and elevators are supplied by the docks. One highly individual profile is provided by the cylindrical deck tanks used to carry liquefied petroleum gas.

Smaller tankers fulfil a coastal service, taking oil from the refineries to the main storage depots, while another family of coasters, short-sea traders and tramps work from harbour to harbour with a range of goods. Many carry their own loading and unloading gear, which allows them a freer choice of ports of call. The cargo-passenger liner is a hybrid and is easily picked out from pure cargo carriers of similar size by the relatively high-level funnel aft of the bridge and the decked accommodation beneath for the passengers. Forward of the bridge, and occupying some two-thirds of the total length, are the cargo holds; two or more derricks are positioned on deck, and the hull may be fitted with side-loading doors to speed the turn-round time in ports.

Dockside view in Hamburg of the P & O supertanker *Ardlui*.

Above: Another of the OCL fleet, the *Resolution Bay*, squeezes through a lock on the Panama Canal. The width of the Canal can determine the dimensions of ships intended for the Far East trade.

CONTAINER SHIPS

The container ship is part of a highly coordinated chain that begins in the factory of origin in one country and ends at the overseas buyer's warehouse which may be on the other side of the world. The system is fairly new and its dependence for success on standardized equipment has provided numerous teething problems, particularly in the early phase in the 1960s when manufacturers, road-haulage and railway companies as well as shipping lines were inclined to adapt existing equipment rather than invest in expensive purpose-built systems.

The idea has many advantages, one of which is that the dispatching and receiving companies can feel more confident that the product should be less subject to damage and pilfering than if it were carried 'loose'. To work efficiently in terms of cost, it is obvious that each container should carry a full load – whether of domestic 'white goods' such as refrigerators, or books, machine parts, or whatever. On arrival at the dockside the container is conveyed by a transporter crane along a travelling gantry and lowered into one of the cellular compartments into which the ship's hold is divided; the retaining walls of the compartments keep the containers in position while at sea. The ship's load may be completed by loading one or two more layers of containers on top of the hatch covers holding down the main cargo. When this is done, the ship's profile takes on an instantly recognizable box-top shape between the bridge and the forecastle.

The size of the containers had been increased after experiment to a maximum length of 40 feet (12·2 metres). Width and height are determined by the dimensions of the road and rail carriers, and are pegged at 8 feet (2·4 metres).

The Roll-on-roll-off principle has its origins in World War II, when the Americans devised a family of specialized landings ships to transport tanks and other vehicles and infantry to the combat area. The inside of a 'Ro-ro' ship operates the principle of a highly compact multi-storey car park. Vehicles bearing containers and self-propelling cargoes such as cars, buses and trucks drive aboard through openings in the bow, stern or side of the ship and are routed by ramps to the appropriate travelling deck. For safety in the event of flooding, vast sliding doors divide the loading area into watertight compartments, and the principal openings are carefully sealed before sailing. The hull is devoted to the role of giant container, and ships of this type usually have a relatively high superstructure aft.

A special feature of the bow- or stern-loading ship are the twin arms of the lifting gear used to raise and lower the ramps. This feature is shared by its smaller relation, the car ferry, familiar to many British holidaymakers driving south in search of the sun, or, in fact, to any foreign country. Britain's position as an island ensures a continuing short-sea ferry trade. In other places, where the crossing is shorter, the time-consuming ferryboat has been discarded for the greater convenience of a multi-span or suspension bridge, the technology for which was largely lacking before the 19th century.

One of the more novel developments in commercial shipping is the ships-within-a-ship system of the LASH vessel. The initials stand for Lighter Aboard Ship. The mother vessel is a kind of self-propelled dock, on to which barges or lighters are lifted by means of a massive travelling crane with legs straddling the stowage space. The cargo-carrying lighters are lined up side by side between bow and stern, and at the journey's end are swung out onto the water and then travel to the unloading dock.

Left: *Liverpool Bay*, a container ship owned by the British group OCL (Overseas Containers Limited), in Hong Kong waters. With a capacity for 2,300 containers, she is almost as long as the *QE2*.

Above: A Union Castle ship, the *Edinburgh Castle* (1948), alongside the Western Docks in Southampton. This line made its reputation on the Cape Town mail service at the turn of the century.

Left: The bulk carrier *Jalatapi* passes across the towering Chicago waterfront.

HYDROFOILS AND HOVERCRAFT

Two systems for reducing contact with the water, and increasing the speed of vessels by this elimination of drag, have found favour in recent years. The hydrofoil adopts the technique of that talented insect the pondskater. The hydrofoils work like the wings of an aircraft: as the ship gains speed, the weight of the hull is progressively transferred to the foils and the vessel lifts off and 'flies'. Difficulties of controlling hydrofoil craft in heavy winds and rough water have limited their use to the generally placid waters of lakes and rivers, but hydrofoils now work passenger routes in such diverse places as the Soviet Union, the Nile and the River Plate in South America. Curiously, the first effective hydrofoil was designed and tested only two years after the Wright brothers in 1903 made the first controlled flight in a powered heavier-than-air machine. The inventor responsible was an Italian, Enrico Forlanini, and his first successful tests were made on Lake Maggiore on the Swiss-Italian border.

Left: 'Flying' passenger hydrofoil in service in the Channel Islands. The potential of these craft is great, though currently limited by problems of handling in high winds and rough water.

Below: Short-sea passenger ship, the *Monte Toledo*, sailing between Southampton and Santander in northern Spain.

Left: The Hoverlloyd vessel *Swift* (1969) on the cross-Channel ferry route between Ramsgate and Calais. This hovercraft can carry 250 passengers and 30 cars, and has a maximum speed of 70 knots.

Left: A specialized vehicle carrier employed by the Renault company for overseas deliveries.

Right: One of Britain's numerous inter-island services — the car and passenger ferry linking the Isle of Skye with the mainland.

Above: A steam-powered dredger at Aviles in northern Spain.

The second breed of 'flier' is the hovercraft, which rides on a cushion of air. This was the invention of Sir Christopher Cockerell, who in the 1950s finally overcame the problems that in the 1870s had defeated the air-cushion vehicle's first proponent, Sir John Thornycroft. The first workable hovercraft, the Saunders-Roe SR–N1, appeared in 1959, and made a Channel crossing on the 50th anniversary of Louis Blériot's record-breaking flight. By this time the hovercraft had taken on the look of present-day Channel ferries using the hover system. Air is pumped beneath the vessel through a slot running round its sides (peripheral jet), it flows towards the centre and provides the necessary lift. The air is contained within the circumference of the vehicle by means of a rubberized skirt. Although, like the hydrofoil, the hovercraft cannot sail in very bad weather, its powers of resilience are being improved, and hoverferries capable of taking vehicles and passengers are in regular service. Hover vehicles capable of speeds in excess of 150 knots are planned. These would be heavy-duty craft able to work in virtually all weathers, and the prospect of crossing the Atlantic in 24 hours is more than a designer's dream.

Right: A Danish Great Belt ferry swallows a passenger train. Between the two sets of rails is a pivoted ramp which rises and falls with the tide.

Above: Harbour tug in New York, used for towage and to help larger ships manoeuvre in confined spaces. A related type is the ocean-going tug which is used for salvage work and long-distance towing – as when Brunel's *Great Britain* was returned to Bristol in 1970 from the Falkland Islands.

Left: An impressive wake carved by an icebreaker working its way along the frozen river Moskva in Moscow.

Alone Against the Oceans

'Ah, but that's yachting,' some seamen might object when asked about solo ocean racing. 'Yachts don't *do* anything.'

The likening of yachts to some admittedly complicated form of toy is perhaps a matter of opinion. Yachts, nowadays, don't *do* anything, in the form of commercial trade. When it was invented in the 17th century by the Dutch, the *jacht* was seen as an inland pleasure craft, though there is little to distinguish it from the early American schooners, which certainly were commerical vessels, and the brigantines that evolved from them.

In 1660 Charles II was presented by the States General of Holland with the 100-ton yacht *Mary*; despite her eight guns she was intended as a pleasure vessel. And in a painting by Abraham Storck, two ships of yacht rig are seen in the array of vessels surrounding the skiff that in 1698 conveyed Peter the Great of Russia round the ships at anchor during his visit to Amsterdam.

Charles II even indulged in some yacht racing himself, taking the helm of his *Katherine* on a course between Greenwich and Gravesend. From this and other evidence Falconer in his *Marine Dictionary* of 1771 compiled the definition of a yacht as 'a vessel of state, usually employed to convey princes, ambassadors or other great personages from one kingdom to another.'

From these beginnings the sport of yacht racing grew, and yachts borrowed from the lines of the revenue cutter and the schooner to make themselves stronger and faster. It is not the purpose of this closing chapter to chart the evolution of the racing yacht, but to look briefly at a phenomenon that has taken hold in the last 20 years – the single-handed voyage, sometimes pursued in competition with others, sometimes done for its own sake.

Improvements in self-steering gear greatly expanded the possibilities for the lone yachtsman. With the feats that they began to achieve came the realization that while yachts may not *do* anything, the men and women sailing them were setting new and exciting targets in human achievement.

Yachts in their early form as pleasure craft welcome Peter the Great on his visit to Amsterdam. This view was painted by Abraham Storck in 1710.

Right: Chief pioneer of single-handed yacht racing in the modern age was Sir Francis Chichester, who in his *Gypsy Moth* series astounded people with his feats in the first *Observer* solo transatlantic race and in his voyage round the world in 1966-67.

Right: Sir Alec Rose, second man of the modern knights of the sea, sailed alone round the world in 1967-68 in a 9-ton cutter, *Lively Lady*. This vessel, like *Gypsy Moth IV*, is now in the collection of the Maritime Trust.

Below: Chay Blyth, who first came to prominence when he rowed across the Atlantic with John Ridgeway, is widely admired among sailors for his feat in sailing round the world the 'wrong' way, i.e. westward against the wind. He made his circumnavigation in *British Steel* in 1970-71 in a record-breaking time of 272 days.

Much of what was to come issued from the first London *Observer* solo transatlantic race, staged in 1960 and won by Francis Chichester. He took 40 days 12 hours 30 minutes and covered 4,004 miles in sailing his sloop *Gypsy Moth III* from Plymouth to New York. It was not a fast time by 1980 standards, but the race seized the public imagination as much as any confrontation of man versus the elements since the Hillary-Tenzing ascent of Mount Everest in 1953. People devoured Chichester's famous book, *The Lonely Sea and the Sky*, when it appeared in 1964, and there followed a spate of solo ocean voyages. It is interesting to look back along those 20 years and see some of the raw excitement that Chichester and others conveyed to the world. One of the most striking things about Chichester's account is the fresh eye with which he managed to view every new crisis as it broke. 'Improvise or die' seems to have been the unspoken motto he worked to on that remarkable voyage.

The first *Observer* race gave Chichester new energy. With his singular blend of the ascetic and the convivial, he fought off his cancer to take part in the 1964 race, and finished second. Then in 1966–67 he sailed alone round the world in the ketch *Gipsy Moth IV*, and was knighted on his return with the same sword used by Elizabeth I to knight Sir Francis Drake in 1581.

While Chichester went on to tackle new barriers, the *Observer* race became a regular four-year fixture, and other round-the-world voyages followed. Next was Alec Rose, a merchant seaman-turned-greengrocer who in 1967–68 sailed his nine-ton cutter *Lively Lady* from Portsmouth to Melbourne via the Cape of Good Hope and returned to Portsmouth after rounding Cape Horn.

Then it was the turn of Robin Knox-Johnston to capture the headlines by winning the London *Sunday Times* solo non-stop voyage round the world.

Robin Knox-Johnston has captured quantities of headlines for his solo voyages. One of the best documented was his 1968-69 non-stop circumnavigation in a race sponsored by the London *Sunday Times*. He was the only one of seven starters to finish.

Right: Outstanding among the women who have ventured to sea alone is Naomi James. With barely a couple of seasons' sailing experience behind her, she set out to sail round the world – non-stop, single-handed and in record time. She was made a Dame Commander of the Order of the British Empire for her achievements.

Above: Currently most successful of the long-distance yachtsmen is a Frenchman, Eric Tabarley, commander of the *Pen Duick* series.

That was in 1968–69, and Knox-Johnston went on to prove himself a remarkable competitor in other events. Women, too, have been eager to show that generally smaller muscles and bodyweight do not disqualify them from the fierce challenges of solo voyaging. Naomi James is one who has broken through, while the jutting-jawed Clare Francis has become one of Britain's most famous sportswomen. After sailing round the world with others, she too joined the transatlantic racers, and brought her experiences into the world's living rooms by recording a spoken log and filming herself as she sailed.

Currently the most eminent solo voyager must be the Frenchman Eric Tabarly. With his series of *Pen Duick* vessels he has dominated in the Atlantic and in the Pacific. In 1969 he sailed some 5,300 miles in less than 40 days to win the Transpacific race from San Francisco to Tokyo.

The records go on tumbling year after year. Speed, though, is not the ultimate object. It is something deeper, more personal; to take on the ocean, and come to terms with it, changes people.